The New Rural Poverty

Philip Martin, Michael Fix, and
J. Edward Taylor

Also of interest from the Urban Institute Press:

Black Males Left Behind, edited by Ronald B. Mincy

Reconnecting Disadvantaged Young Men, by Peter Edelman, Harry J.
Holzer, and Paul Offner

Health Policy and the Uninsured, edited by Catherine G. McLaughlin

AGRICULTURE & IMMIGRATION IN CALIFORNIA

The New Rural Poverty

PHILIP MARTIN, MICHAEL FIX, & J. EDWARD TAYLOR

THE URBAN INSTITUTE PRESS
Washington, D.C.

THE URBAN INSTITUTE PRESS
2100 M Street, N.W.
Washington, D.C. 20037

Library of Congress Cataloging-in-Publication Data

Martin, Philip L., 1949–
  The new rural poverty : agriculture and immigration in California / Philip Martin, Michael Fix, and J. Edward Taylor.
     p. cm.
  Includes bibliographical references and index.
  ISBN 0-87766-729-2 (alk. paper)
  1. Migrant agricultural laborers--United States.   2. Rural poor--United States.
3. Alien labor, Mexican--United States.   4. Agriculture--United States.   5. United
States--Rural conditions.   I. Fix, Michael.   II. Taylor, J. Edward.   III. Title.
  HD1525.N48   2006
  331.5'440973--dc22

                                                                          2005035512

Printed in the United States of America

10 09 08 07 06   1 2 3 4 5

THE URBAN INSTITUTE is a nonprofit, nonpartisan policy research and educational organization established in Washington, D.C., in 1968. Its staff investigates the social, economic, and governance problems confronting the nation and evaluates the public and private means to alleviate them. The Institute disseminates its research findings through publications, its web site, the media, seminars, and forums.

Through work that ranges from broad conceptual studies to administrative and technical assistance, Institute researchers contribute to the stock of knowledge available to guide decisionmaking in the public interest.

Conclusions or opinions expressed in Institute publications are those of the authors and do not necessarily reflect the views of officers or trustees of the Institute, advisory groups, or any organizations that provide financial support to the Institute.

CONTENTS

PREFACE

Rural poverty has been the subject of some of America's best known literature, including John Steinbeck's *The Grapes of Wrath*, which chronicled the reception that Dust Bowl migrants received in California in the 1930s. Reports of "the people left behind," such as Michael Harrington's *The Other America*, helped to inspire the War on Poverty in the 1960s by calling attention to an invisible, enduring rural poverty.

The rural poverty associated with small farms and sharecroppers for most of the 20th century diminished but did not disappear. Meanwhile, a new type of poverty has appeared in rural and agricultural areas with the arrival of rural Mexicans to fill farm and farm-related jobs. Most of the Mexicans who begin their American journeys as seasonal farmworkers remain in the fields for less than a decade, and their children educated in the United States do not follow their parents into the fields.

This combination of high farmworker attrition and low reproduction of U.S. farmworkers poses a dilemma for rural America. Farmers argue that migrants are needed to sustain and expand agriculture and related industries. However, if newcomers seeking the American dream remain farmworkers for a decade or less, and their children shun farm jobs, rural America becomes an immigration treadmill, serving as a port of entry for newcomers but not providing careers for the immigrants and their children. Immigrants too old to fill farm jobs, and their children who refuse them, could become a new rural underclass, one whose only opportunity for mobility will require migration to urban areas.

The new rural poverty results from expanding labor-intensive fresh fruit and vegetable production and rising Mexico–United States migration. Both processes were accelerated, perhaps unintentionally, by diverse trends, including affluence, healthier diets, and immigration reforms in the mid-1980s and the North American Free Trade Agreement (NAFTA) a decade later. In the 1960s, no one expected the number of farmworkers to increase, especially after the bracero program ended and the fledgling United Farm Workers union pushed the wages of some California farmworkers to twice the federal minimum wage, spurring a wave of harvest mechanization (O'Brien, Cargill, and Fridley 1983). However, instead of a mechanized agriculture employing fewer and better paid workers, production of hand-picked commodities such as strawberries and broccoli expanded, and the availability of migrants and farm jobs reinforced one another's growth. Migrant workers enabled farmers to plant broccoli or other crops and assume that harvest workers would be available, and expanding harvest jobs encouraged rural Mexicans suffering from peso devaluations and economic restructuring to migrate to the United States.

Legalization of migrant workers and employer sanctions in the late 1980s were expected to return agriculture to the 1960s era of rising wages and mechanization. However, only one side of this legalization and enforcement "grand bargain" was implemented. The farmworker legalization program, often considered rife with fraud, gave immigrant status to a sixth of the adult men in rural Mexico, but employer sanctions were not enforced and did little to stem the flow of unauthorized Mexicans, who obtained fraudulent documents and jobs. Contrary to expectations, many newly legalized Mexicans brought their families to the United States instead of shuttling between seasonal U.S. farm jobs and homes in Mexico, literally changing the face of the U.S. areas in which they settled.

Some of the Mexicans who settled in the United States found upward mobility by leaving California farm fields and moving to midwestern and southeastern towns and cities to fill jobs in farm-related industries. Meat and poultry plants seeking additional workers, as well as construction contractors and hotels and restaurants, often hired a pioneer migrant seeking year-round work and lower housing costs. After the migrant proved to be a good worker, the employer asked him to bring family and friends to fill vacant jobs, and soon migrants moved directly from rural Mexico to such cities as Storm Lake, Iowa, and Rogers, Arkansas. Workers from particular Mexican villages soon dominated harvesting and factory crews in some U.S. workplaces, and information on job vacancies sometimes traveled faster to rural Mexico than to nearby U.S. labor markets.

The wages of newcomer migrants are high by Mexican standards but low by U.S. standards, so the same immigration flows that preserve farm and farm-related industries in rural America are also increasing poverty in many of these new migration destinations. This new rural poverty is the focus of this book. We explain how agriculture became dependent on immigrant workers, how immigration and integration patterns are playing out in specific rural communities and commodities, and the relationship between farm employment, immigration, and poverty. We also explore the policy options to reduce the risk that current Mexico–United States migration will simply transfer poverty from rural Mexico to rural America.

The Changing Face project is a unique collaboration between think tank researchers and academics. We began the project in 1995 with the support of the Rosenberg Foundation and received additional support from the S.H. Cowell, Farm, Giannini, and Kellogg Foundations, as well as from the United States Department of Agriculture under a national research initiative grant. We wish to acknowledge the information and encouragement we received from the farm employers, local leaders, and migrants and their supporters who participated in our seminars and informed us during field trips. We dedicate this book to them and hope that it provides a road map to those grappling with questions that have no easy answers.

This book is organized as follows. Part 1 has three chapters that outline the interdependencies between immigrants and agriculture. Part 2 examines the changing face of rural America in three areas: inland agricultural valleys in California, farm areas in coastal California, and meat and poultry processing centers in Delaware and Iowa. Part 3 turns to the policy challenges and options, assessing the likely impacts of current proposals for immigration reform on rural America. We conclude with the fundamental question, Is one solution to rising farm-worker poverty in the 21st century to ensure that migrants are guest workers who eventually return to their countries of origin, as President Bush proposes, or can seasonal farmwork be a first step up the U.S. job ladder?

PART 1

IMPORTING MIGRANTS, IMPORTING POVERTY

The three chapters in part 1 explore the changing face of rural America. Chapter 1 explores the major policy options, emphasizing that the U.S. government has traditionally made exceptions in its immigration laws for farmers to obtain foreign workers. The question is whether these foreign workers should be guests expected to leave the United States or immigrants who settle and whose children may need help to escape from seasonal farmwork. Chapter 2 explains that seasonality has always been the core labor issue in agriculture, and that the dependence of agriculture on migrants has spread from the western states to the rest of U.S. agriculture. Chapter 3 makes the relationship among agricultural expansion, immigration, and poverty more precise, showing that the availability of migrants allows farmers to expand production of fruits and vegetables, and that the arrival of migrants to fill the resulting seasonal jobs increases the number of poor working families in rural America.

1

IMMIGRANTS AND 21ST CENTURY AGRICULTURE

The face of rural America is changing as a result of immigration, primarily from Mexico. From Florida to Washington and from Maine to California, migrants arrive in agricultural areas to fill jobs on farms and in such farm-related industries as meat processing. Many of these areas have relatively small populations, so newcomers are often very visible in places that have not experienced significant immigration for over a century. Most newcomers are not authorized to work in the United States, and this illegality complicates the quest for policy options that preserve traditional industries in rural America.

The story of how 21st century rural America has become home to these typically poorly educated newcomers began almost 140 years ago, when the completion of the transcontinental railroad in 1869 made it feasible to produce fruits and vegetables in California and other western states for East Coast consumers. Most Americans wanted to own the land they farmed or work year-round in urban areas, so seasonal farmwork became jobs of last resort for newcomers who could not become farmers or get "regular" jobs. Waves of newcomers without other U.S. job options—Chinese, Japanese, and South Asian migrants before World War I, Mexicans and Filipinos in the 1920s, Dust Bowl refugees in the 1930s, and braceros in the 1940s and 1950s—accepted seasonal farm jobs but soon sought something better for themselves and their children.[1]

Farm labor reformers decried the poverty associated with seasonal farmwork, and after the publication of *The Grapes of Wrath* in April

1940, President Franklin Roosevelt said that "something must be done and done soon" to improve conditions for migrant and seasonal farmworkers (quoted in Martin 2003, 46). However, before the minimum wage and collective bargaining laws that were a core of the New Deal could be extended to farmworkers, World War II broke out, and farmers argued that, without additional workers, there would not be sufficient food to win the war.

Instead of enacting new protective laws for farmworkers that could have made farmwork a "regular" job, the United States and Mexico negotiated a guest worker program—the bracero program—which admitted almost 4.5 million Mexican farmworkers before its end in 1964, which coincided with the civil rights movement and the War on Poverty. With new nonfarm job options available to previously excluded Americans came the supposed end to the revolving door system under which U.S. workers and newcomers accepted seasonal farm jobs until they could find something better. Indeed, there was a brief golden era for farmworkers between the mid-1960s and late 1970s, when Cesar Chavez was featured on the cover of *Time* and farm wages rose to twice the federal minimum wage under the United Farm Workers' union contracts. In response to rising wages, many farmers mechanized manual jobs, the University of California developed a mechanical tomato harvester, and there were literally hundreds of experiments on mechanically harvesting apples, oranges, and lettuce.

This era of rising farm wages and mechanization ended in the early 1980s, when Mexico devalued the peso and farmers turned to labor contractors who recruited Mexican workers, many undocumented. At that time, there were no penalties for U.S. employers that knowingly hired unauthorized workers. Enforcement of immigration laws consisted of the Border Patrol driving into fields and trying to apprehend workers who ran from them, an ineffective way to discourage the entry and employment of unauthorized workers. Hundreds of thousands of Mexicans headed north, slowing wage increases and reducing farmers' incentives to invest in labor-saving mechanization research.

When discussions of immigration reforms that might slow the influx of unauthorized workers became more serious in the mid-1980s, farm employers worried. In 1983–84, an estimated 20 percent of the 2.5 million individuals employed on U.S. farms were unauthorized. The expectation was that a combination of legalization that permitted migrants to find nonfarm jobs more easily and sanctions on employers that hired illegal workers would bring about dramatic changes, including another round of farm wage increases and more mechanization. However, as often happens with immigration reforms, some unanticipated impacts of the Immigration Reform and Control Act (IRCA) of 1986 outlasted the expected effects.[2] IRCA was expected to discourage unauthorized entries because migrants who successfully entered the United States would not be able to find jobs with employers fearful of fines, while legalized farmworkers could join unions and bargain for wage increases (Commission on Agricultural Workers 1993; Martin 1994).

IRCA legalized 1.2 million foreign farmworkers, 90 percent of whom were Mexican (U.S. Immigration and Naturalization Service 1991). As legal immigrants, these "special agricultural workers" could travel freely, and Mexican farmworkers soon moved from their traditional bases in California, Texas, and Florida to locations throughout the United States. More important, stepped-up border controls failed to discourage young men in rural Mexico from trying to enter the United States illegally, but they did make illegal entry more expensive and dangerous and kept those who entered successfully in the United States longer. The employer sanctions meant to close the labor market door to unauthorized workers failed, largely because it was easy for unauthorized workers to obtain false documents and for employers to escape penalties by copying these documents and asserting that they did not know the documents were false. In addition, the priority placed on enforcing sanctions within the Immigration and Naturalization Service (INS) fell soon after the law's enactment. In the two decades since IRCA's enactment, the share of unauthorized farmworkers has tripled to about 60 percent of all farmworkers (Carroll et al. 2005).

During the early 1990s recession, the costs of providing public services to illegal immigrants and their U.S.-born children became a major issue. California and other states sued the federal government to recoup their costs of providing services to the illegal immigrant population. Farm employers, civic leaders, and migrant organizations reported an upsurge in migrants unifying their families in rural and agricultural areas across the United States,[3] a change from the pattern described by folksinger Woody Guthrie as migrants coming with the dust and going with the wind. Settled migrants sought housing, education for their children, and health care, often in rural areas not prepared to integrate newcomers.

THE CHALLENGE

The immigration and integration challenges facing the United States are profound. Since 1990, the number of foreign-born U.S. residents has doubled, to 35 million, and a third of the newcomers are from Mexico. At least half of the 5 million Mexicans entering in the 1990s had their first U.S. job in rural and agricultural areas, and this fact raises the questions that we explore in this book: is the United States re-creating rural poverty by allowing farmers to hire migrants whose seasonal employment leaves them with below–poverty level earnings? Will newcomers from rural Mexico who begin their American journeys in agriculture be able to climb the U.S. farm ladder from worker to owner, or will economic mobility in the United States require occupational and geographic mobility, so farmworkers and their children have to become non-farmworkers to get ahead?

The Changing Face project has spent a decade in the rural and agricultural areas that attract newcomers from rural Mexico. Employers reported that, without a steady stream of newcomers, they could not pick their apples or oranges, process pigs or chickens, or build new homes. Mayors, police chiefs, and teachers emphasized that integration was proceeding unevenly, as many migrants and their children were achieving some version of the American dream of higher wages and more opportunities, but others found persistent poverty, overcrowded housing, and the type of gang activity associated with urban areas. Migrants were generally hopeful, but many noted that it was much harder than they expected to get ahead in the United States.

Policy Issues and Options

Three major facts frame the challenges facing a demographically changing rural America. One, many farmers, meatpackers, and leaders of other rural industries are adamant that, without a steady influx of foreign workers, they could not survive. Two, rural Mexico still has too many people; agriculture in Mexico employs about 20 percent of all workers but generates only 5 percent of gross domestic product, and widespread poverty encourages emigration. Three, one legacy of the bracero and IRCA legalization programs, as well as the sustained high levels of unauthorized migration, has been to forge links between rural Mexico and rural America that are hard to break.

A set of policy options flows from these facts. If the United States decides to satisfy the demand for labor in rural and agricultural areas rather than reduce it with subsidized mechanization or freer trade that lowers prices and forces some farmers out of business, then the question becomes how to minimize the immigration and integration challenges associated with current migration patterns. Proposed policy primarily targets two types of migrants: those already in the United States illegally and those yet to come. Two competing policy visions predominate. President Bush wants to turn unauthorized foreigners with U.S. employers into guest workers and to reduce illegal immigration in the future by opening new channels for legal guest worker admissions. An alternative, bipartisan proposal would make currently unauthorized foreigners probationary immigrants and would allow them and their families to become immigrants if they satisfy conditions such as paying taxes and learning English.

Guest workers, legalization, and earned legalization dominate the immigration policy debate. However, even if one of these reforms is adopted, the question remains of what to do about the migrants already in rural areas. Should the assistance programs that were developed in the 1960s to deal with migrant U.S. farmworkers and their children be sustained to help newcomers from rural Mexico and their children in rural America? Should federal and state policies that affect immigrant integration, ranging from the No Child Left Behind Act to health programs for poor residents, be modified for agricultural areas that may lack people to implement them or economies of scale in service delivery?

The Changing Face project is a bottom-up effort to evaluate the trade-offs involved in relying on migrant newcomers to fill seasonal farm jobs. We have tried to present fairly the views of the employers, city leaders, and migrants and their advocates in this book, and we hope that readers will appreciate the difficulties involved in deciding whether the good of preserving decades-old industries outweighs the competing good of limiting poverty in rural towns.

2

MIGRANTS IN U.S. AGRICULTURE

The first U.S. Census of Population in 1790 found that 90 percent of the 4 million U.S. residents lived in rural areas, where most adults were farmers or farmworkers. Family farming was a way of life as well as a business that supported farmers and their families. In the view of so-called agrarian fundamentalists, farming was both an essential business and a virtuous way of life to be fostered and encouraged. Thomas Jefferson, the third U.S. president, considered family farmers the backbone of American democracy. In his 1782 *Notes on Virginia*, Jefferson wrote, "Those who labor in the earth are the chosen people of God . . . . corruption of morals in the mass of cultivators is a phenomenon of which no age or nation has furnished an example" (quoted in Limerick 1987, 58). Jefferson believed that rural life was superior to urban life and that self-sufficient family farmers would preserve fledgling American democracy.

Family farms were the ideal as well as the reality for most of American agriculture. The model family farm included a hard-working farmer, his family, and a hired hand, a young man who lived with the farmer's family and perhaps married the farmer's daughter, one reason why 19th century reports drew no distinctions between farmers and farmworkers (Daniel 1981). Everyone on family farms worked to meet peak seasonal labor needs, and children went to school during the winter months. Seasonality encouraged diversification to achieve self-sufficiency and spread out the demand for labor, which is why most family farms both raised crops and tended livestock.

Two other farming systems, plantations based on slaves and commercial farms dependent on migrants, represented very different responses to the seasonal demand for labor inherent in agriculture. Plantations in the southern states specialized in the production of labor-intensive cotton and tobacco, and on a scale too great for even large farm families to provide all the labor. Growing seasons were six to eight months, helping to justify paying the upkeep of slaves year-round to ensure that they were available for seasonal farmwork. Most plantations had at least 20 slaves and 400 acres of cotton. The price of slaves, $500 to $1,000 for an adult male, fluctuated with the prices of tobacco and cotton (Fogel and Engerman 1974). During the 18th and 19th centuries, slavery spread westward in the southern states, where long-season crops were grown and labor-intensive crops such as cotton and sugar were cultivated.

In contrast to the southern plantation, where hired hands and slaves both lived on the farms on which they worked, the newer commercial agriculture of the western states relied on wage workers that migrated from farm to farm. The key to unlocking the potential of western agriculture was the transcontinental railroad, which lowered transportation costs and interest rates and integrated the western states into the U.S. economy (Fuller 1939/1940). Farmers who had previously needed thousands of acres to operate farms on which they sowed seed in the fall and harvested wheat in the spring (if there were sufficient rains) now had an incentive to invest in irrigation systems and plant trees that would produce fruit for eastern consumers. To have the seasonal labor force needed for fruit farming, large dryland grain farms were expected to be broken up into family-sized units (Fuller 1939/1940).

Because migrant workers were available, however, large western farms did not have to be subdivided into family-sized units to support the workers needed for more labor-intensive fruit cultivation. The first significant group of migrant farm laborers was the Chinese, who had been imported to build the railroad. After being laid off, they drifted into such cities as San Francisco and Sacramento, where they faced discrimination from white workers, many of whom also lost their jobs when the railroad brought lower-cost manufactured goods from the East. Shut out of city jobs, the Chinese represented 75 percent of seasonal farmworkers in California by the early 1880s (Fuller 1939/1940). Since the Chinese were paid only when they worked, farmers saved money on wages. Low wage costs made farming more profitable and thus raised land prices. The continued arrival of newcomers willing to be seasonal workers was thus in the landowners' interest.

Nevertheless, there was widespread opposition to an agricultural system dependent on migrant workers. Chinese immigration stopped in 1882, and a governor's report a few years later noted approvingly that "a great revolution is taking place, whereby the larger land holdings are breaking up, and being sold . . . in small tracts to families that are seeking homes" (quoted in Daniel 1981, 33). However, aspiring family farmers who did their own work earned the equivalent of what was paid to Chinese workers employed seasonally, and many soon abandoned farming for nonfarm jobs. Meanwhile, the Chinese workers aged, and farmers worried about who would take their place doing seasonal farmwork.

Farmers found another source of seasonal workers in Japan, which legalized emigration in 1885 to relieve population pressures. Japanese migration to the United States peaked between 1901 and 1907, when 130,000 arrived. Half of these Japanese immigrants became farmworkers (Fuller 1939/1940, 19829). The Japanese were the only group from which significant numbers of seasonal workers climbed the agricultural ladder from worker to farmer, owing in part to their willingness to mount harvest-time strikes, work for a share of the crop rather than for wages, and buy marginal farmland to produce vegetables that were sold directly to consumers. This competition made California farmers ambivalent about Japanese workers, and they did not oppose a 1907 "gentlemen's agreement" that stopped Japanese immigration.[1]

After the Japanese, western farmers turned to what is now India and Pakistan for workers under the theory that, as British subjects, "Hindu" farmworkers[2] could be admitted despite the general ban on Asian immigrants. Many "Hindus" abandoned seasonal farmwork to become small farmers, prompting recruitment drives among U.S. blacks in the Southeast and American Indians on reservations. Partly because of these successful efforts to find newcomers willing to be seasonal workers, most European immigrants at the beginning of the 20th century avoided California.[3] An estimated 100,000 of the 12 million European immigrants who arrived between 1900 and 1914 came to California (Martin 2003, ch. 2).

During World War I, many seasonal workers went into the military or into wartime industries, and a labor supply crisis loomed. Western farmers, who were still expanding their production of labor-intensive crops with new irrigation facilities and improved transportation systems, asked the U.S. Department of Labor (DOL) "to admit temporarily otherwise inadmissible aliens" to do farmwork. This first bracero program admitted 51,000 Mexican guest workers between 1917 and 1921 but left the Mexican government dissatisfied because many braceros experienced discrimination in the United States (Fuller 1939/1940, 19853). Some Mexican migrants wound up with little in savings because of the charges they incurred at the farmer-owned stores and camps.

The United States' immigration policy, which facilitated immigration before the 1880s, imposed qualitative restrictions in the 1880s (such as no Chinese immigrants) and adopted quantitative limits in the 1920s that favored immigration from northern and western Europe. However, these quantitative limits did not apply to Mexico and other Western Hemisphere countries, and there was no U.S. Border Patrol until 1924, so Mexicans seeking jobs could enter the United States with few obstacles. Farmers helped to defeat efforts in Congress to restrict immigration from Mexico by arguing that western agriculture needed seasonal migrants and that Mexicans would return to Mexico. One California farm representative told Congress in 1926 that "We, gentlemen, are just as anxious as you are not to build the civilization of California or any other western district upon a Mexican foundation. We take him because there is nothing else available. We have gone east, west, north, and south and he is the only man-power available to us" (quoted in Fuller 1939/1940, 19859).

Reformers argued that, if farmers paid workers higher wages and offered them jobs as year-round hired hands, they could find U.S. workers. Farmers countered that they could not raise wages and could afford to pay workers only for the season worked. One farmer said that if "we should be forced to maintain our [farm] labor when it is idle, we would be forced out of business" (Fuller 1939/1940, 19864). Mexicans were the ideal seasonal workers because they were "homing pigeons" who returned to Mexico every winter (Fuller 1939/1940, 19859).

The 1930s saw an outpouring of books and reports on the plight of farmworkers in California and other western states, but there were no significant changes in the farm labor market. California had 5.7 million residents in 1930, and Dust Bowl migration brought 1.3 million midwestern Okies and Arkies to the state, increasing the population by 25 percent. Dust Bowl migrants drove up to farmhouses and asked for work, expecting to be treated as Jeffersonian hired hands who lived on the farm where they worked and who would eventually climb the ladder from worker to farmer. Instead of becoming hired hands, many wound up in tent camps known as Hoovervilles, prompting concern that white English-speaking migrants could become a fertile breeding ground for Communist organizers.[4]

Two congressional committees examined farm labor conditions. Both agreed that there were severe problems, but they reached opposing conclusions about what to do. The House Committee on Un-American Activities warned that Communists were establishing unions among seasonal workers and urged stepped-up law enforcement to counter the Communists. The Senate's Education and Labor Committee, on the other hand, urged the federal government to extend collective bargaining rights to farmworkers so that they could form and join unions to raise their wages.

Because of this disagreement and the outbreak of World War II, Congress did not act on farm labor conditions. Instead of enacting legislation that could have led to higher farm wages, Congress approved a new bracero program in 1942 that kept a lid on wages. However, at the insistence of the Mexican government, the U.S. government guaranteed the contracts farmers provided to Mexican workers, ensuring that braceros received their wages (Craig 1971). Between 1942 and 1964, the United States had some 4.6 million bracero admissions (table 2.1). Many returned year after year, and the 1 to 2 million who participated gained U.S. work experience that proved valuable when the program ended (U.S. Senate Committee 1980).

Despite the opportunity to migrate legally, more Mexicans were apprehended during the bracero years than came legally, 5.3 million versus 4.6 million (both admissions and apprehensions count more than once individuals admitted or apprehended several times). The reason for illegal migration alongside legal guest workers is clear: Mexicans had an incentive to migrate outside the program to avoid paying bribes in Mexico to get on recruitment lists, while U.S. employ-

Table 2.1. Mexican Bracero Admissions, Apprehensions, and Immigrants, 1942–64

Year	Braceros	Apprehensions	Immigrants
1942	4,203	11,784	2,378
1943	52,098	11,175	4,172
1944	62,170	31,174	6,598
1945	49,454	69,164	6,702
1946	32,043	99,591	7,146
1947	19,632	193,657	7,558
1948	35,345	192,779	8,384
1949	107,000	288,253	8,803
1950	67,500	468,339	6,744
1951	192,000	509,040	6,153
1952	197,100	528,815	9,079
1953	201,380	885,587	17,183
1954	309,033	1,089,583	30,645
1955	398,650	254,096	43,702
1956	445,197	87,696	61,320
1957	436,049	59,918	49,321
1958	432,857	53,474	26,721
1959	437,643	45,336	22,909
1960	315,846	70,684	32,708
1961	291,420	88,823	41,476
1962	194,978	92,758	55,805
1963	186,865	88,712	55,986
1964	177,736	86,597	34,448
Total	4,646,199	5,307,035	545,941

Source: U.S. Congress, Senate Committee on the Judiciary (1980).
Note: Bracero admissions and apprehensions are events, not unique individuals.

ers had an incentive to hire Mexicans who simply showed up to avoid having to pay travel costs from the workers' place of recruitment, which could be far inside Mexico.

There were few penalties on workers or employers operating outside the bracero program. Mexicans discovered working illegally in the United States were often legalized in a process official U.S. government publications called "drying out the wetbacks" (President's Commission on Migratory Labor 1951). They were taken to the Mexico–U.S. border, documented, and then returned to the farm on which they were found, with no penalties imposed on their employer.

The President's Commission on Migratory Labor in 1951 concluded that braceros and illegal workers held down U.S. farm wages, and urged that conditions for U.S. workers be improved by reducing the employment of braceros, extending minimum wage and union protections to farmworkers, and reducing illegal immigration by sanctioning farmers who hired illegal workers. U.S. President Truman and Mexican President Miguel Aleman agreed, and the Mexican government asserted that "the wetback exodus could be stopped only when [U.S.] employers were penalized for hiring them" (Craig 1971, 75). However, farmers opposed to sanctions prevailed in Congress, and the Immigration and Nationality Act of 1952 included the so-called Texas proviso: "harboring" illegal aliens was a felony, but employing unauthorized workers was explicitly defined as not harboring them.

Braceros' admissions and apprehensions rose together in the early 1950s, when U.S. Attorney General Herbert Brownwell toured the Mexico–United States border and pronounced himself "shocked" by the lawlessness he observed there. He appointed ex-general Joseph Swing INS commissioner and ordered him to "clean up" the border (Martin 2003, ch. 2). Swing launched "Operation Wetback" in June 1954, quickly removing 1.1 million Mexicans, including some unauthorized Mexicans' children who were born in the United States and thus were U.S. citizens. These stepped-up efforts to apprehend unauthorized Mexicans were coupled with a DOL policy that relaxed regulations requiring farmers to provide approved housing. The result was more bracero admissions, 445,197 in 1956 (12 percent more than in 1955), and fewer apprehensions, 87,696 in 1956 (one-third the number in 1955).

During the 1950s, the availability of braceros allowed labor-intensive agriculture to expand without raising wages significantly.[5] As California replaced New Jersey as the garden state of the United States, numerous commissions and reports criticized farmers for mistreating and underpaying both braceros and U.S. workers, such as the CBS documentary *Harvest of Shame* in November 1960. Mexican Americans, who mostly lived in rural and agricultural areas in 1950, migrated in large numbers to such cities as San Jose and Los Angeles by 1960. Criticism by unions, churches, and researchers persuaded DOL to step up its enforcement of wage and housing standards. Growers responded to higher wages and tougher conditions by mechanizing the harvesting of cotton and the thinning of sugar beets (DOL 1959).

The election of President Kennedy in 1960 further strengthened DOL enforcement of bracero program rules, and protesting farmers almost succeeded in having administration of the program transferred to the U.S. Department of Agriculture (California Senate 1961, 1963). Churches, unions, and Hispanic groups convinced Kennedy that braceros were "adversely affecting the wages, working conditions, and employment opportunities of our own agricultural workers," and tried to end the program in 1961. However, he agreed to a two-year extension because of the "serious impact in Mexico if thousands of workers employed in this country were summarily deprived of this much-needed employment" (Craig 1971, 172–73). The showdown in Congress came in 1963, and farmers may have won another extension of the bracero program but for a tragedy in Chualar in the Salinas Valley (Galarza 1977), when 32 braceros died in September 1963 after their bus collided with a train. Their bodies were not claimed immediately because farmers and contractors argued over who was responsible for them. The accident strengthened the hand of those who argued the program was out of control, and Congress voted for a final one-year extension, until December 31, 1964.

From Unions to IRCA

The year 1965 was a year of transition for labor-intensive U.S. agriculture, with some farmers responding by using seasonal workers more efficiently and others mechanizing. USDA estimated that the number of U.S. migrants who followed the crops around the United States rose to a record 465,000, or 15 percent of the 3.1 million hired farmworkers (Smith and Coltrane 1981). To better manage the fewer workers available, some farmers joined or formed co-ops that deployed workers in a manner that minimized unemployment, aiming to develop a core group of professional seasonal workers who had higher earnings because they could work more hours as the co-op moved them from farm to farm. One lemon harvesting cooperative, for example, downsized from 8,000 workers in 1965 to 1,200 in the early 1970s and tripled average worker earnings by making screening and deployment more efficient (Lloyd, Martin, and Mamer 1988).

There was also a wave of labor-saving mechanization in crops that had depended on bracero workers (O'Brien et al. 1983). In the early 1960s, about 80 percent of the peak 45,000 workers who handpicked the tomatoes for ketchup were braceros. Tomato farmers and the processors who had invested in plants to produce tomato products were adamant that "the use of braceros is absolutely essential to the survival of the tomato industry" (U.S. House Committee 1963, 60). The director of the California Department of Agriculture testified in support of extending the program by arguing that, without braceros, "we could expect a 50 percent decrease in the production of tomatoes" in California (Ibid., 61).

The tomato farmers and their supporters turned out to be wrong. Today, about 5,000 local workers operate machines that harvest 11 million tons of tomatoes, five times more than during the bracero era. Mechanization proceeded faster than expected, as plant scientists developed tomatoes that ripened at the same time and had an oblong shape amenable to mechanical harvesting and bulk handling, while engineers developed a machine capable of cutting tomato plants, shaking the tomatoes off the vines, and conveying them past sorters riding on the machine who picked out debris before conveyors carried the tomatoes to twin 12.5-ton tubs pulled alongside the machine. The harvested tomatoes were checked for quality at state-run random sampling stations[6] and then taken to canneries for processing. In less than a decade, California tomatoes transformed from a handpicked to a machine-picked industry (table 2.2).

There were many consequences of tomato harvest mechanization, and some curtailed mechanization research. The number of harvest workers fell sharply, as did the number of farms growing tomatoes, since tomato harvesting machines were costly, forcing farmers to spe-

Table 2.2. California Processing Tomatoes, 1960–74

Year	Acres	Production (million tons)	Machine-harvested (%)
1960	130,000	2,249	0
1961	146,800	2,319	0
1962	177,200	3,218	1
1963	129,000	2,463	2
1964	143,000	3,003	4
1965	122,800	2,468	25
1966	162,500	3,136	66
1967	186,700	3,192	82
1968	231,300	4,903	95
1969	154,000	3,373	100
1970	141,300	3,363	100
1971	163,700	3,880	100
1972	178,900	4,526	100
1973	218,000	4,861	100
1974	249,900	6,040	100

Source: California Department of Food and Agriculture (2005).

cialize. These worker and farmer impacts prompted suits against the University of California, the developer of the plants and machine, alleging that taxpayer monies should help all rural residents, not just large and specialized tomato farms (Martin and Olmstead 1985). Harvest mechanization research was put on hold while the suit was pending and did not resume in the 1980s, in part because unauthorized workers were readily available.

A third effect of the bracero program's termination, besides fewer farms and workers, was a new wave of union activities. There had been efforts to organize farmworkers throughout the 20th century, but most unions proved short-lived, often surviving less than five years (Martin 2003, ch. 3). However, unions seeking members targeted the millions of farmworkers who had lower than average wages. The American Federation of Labor and Congress of Industrial Organizations (AFL-CIO) gave the Agricultural Workers Organizing Committee (AWOC) some of its most successful nonfarm organizers and announced in 1959 that AWOC was on its way to a two-million-member strong union. Because of bracero competition in the fields, AWOC was largely unsuccessful, and in 1965 it included only a few thousand members, including aging Filipino grape pickers who spent the winter on farms in the Delano, California area.

In 1964, braceros received a minimum wage of $1.40 an hour. U.S. farmworkers were not covered by minimum wage legislation, and growers decided in 1965 to reduce the wage paid to U.S. grape pickers to $1.25 an hour. The AWOC-represented Filipinos went on strike and asked the National Farm Workers Association (NFWA), headed by Cesar Chavez, to support their strike. The AWOC-NFWA strike failed to raise wages, but Chavez took over the leadership of the combined group and pioneered a new tactic to put pressure on growers—he called for a boycott during the 1965 Christmas season of the wine and liquor sold by conglomerates that also grew table grapes. The boycott was a success, and in spring 1966,[7] after a march from Delano to Sacramento, the now-named United Farm Workers (UFW) union won a 40 percent wage increase to $1.75 an hour at Schenley Industries, a conglomerate that grew grapes.

The UFW wrote letters to other grape growers announcing that it represented their workers and asked them to sign contracts that raised wages—there was no need for elections because collective bargaining laws excluded farmworkers. Most grape growers ignored the letters, but farmworker issues remained front-page news as churches, unions, students, and politicians boycotted table grapes, lettuce, and wine in support of the UFW. Union activities did not directly affect most growers, but many matched or exceeded union wages to avoid union troubles. Competition between the UFW and the Teamsters union to organize farmworkers, the extension of minimum wage and unemployment insurance protections to farmworkers, and the hiring of nonfarm personnel managers led to predictions that the farm labor market would soon resemble such nonfarm labor markets as construction, which offered higher than average wages to compensate for seasonality. By 1977, the farm–nonfarm wage gap had narrowed significantly as average farmworker earnings reached $3.53 an hour, well above the minimum wage of $2.50 and almost 60 percent of the $6 average in California factories.

However, the immigration seeds planted during the bracero program eventually ended the 1965–80 golden era for farmworkers. Illegal Mexico–United States migration was low during the late 1960s and early 1970s, but Mexicans could become U.S. immigrants if farmers gave them letters offering jobs. These offers of employment enabled tens of thousands of ex-braceros to become "green-card commuters" who kept their families in Mexico and worked seasonally on U.S. farms. By the late 1970s, these green-card commuters were getting too old to be seasonal harvest workers, and some became foremen and contractors who could recruit their sons and other young Mexicans for U.S. farm jobs at a time when peso devaluations made U.S. jobs more attractive than Mexican jobs.

The UFW's successes at the bargaining table came from threatening consumer boycotts, and the UFW was well aware of the threat posed by contractors hiring unauthorized Mexican workers. The UFW testified in support of a larger Border Patrol and employer sanctions but made a strategic error in 1979. In that year, the UFW called a strike in support of its demand for a 42 percent increase in entry-level wages from $3.70 to $5.25 an hour in the Imperial Valley, which borders Mexico in southeastern California. Growers turned to labor contractors who hired unauthorized Mexican workers, prompting Chavez to complain that "employers go to Mexico and have unlimited, unrestricted use of illegal alien strikebreakers to break the strike" (U.S. Senate Committee 1979, 5).

The UFW seemed to win its largest-ever strike when several employers raised wages 40 to 50 percent in summer 1979. However, after signing record farm labor contracts, many of the conglomerates most vulnerable to consumer boycotts stopped farming, and the independent growers who replaced them were far less vulnerable to boycott pressures. UFW membership fell from 70,000 in 1977 to 7,000 by 1985 as farm wages stagnated, benefits such as health insurance disappeared, and farm labor contractors employing crews of newly arrived unauthorized workers proliferated.

IRCA AND THE CHANGING FACE

Lawmakers expected the Immigration Reform and Control Act of 1986 to reverse the downward trend in farm wages and union membership. IRCA was based on a grand bargain of sanctions and legalization. To satisfy those who thought the top priority should be enforcement to discourage unauthorized migration, IRCA included sanctions or fines on employers that knowingly hired unauthorized workers. However, to avoid roundups such as those of the early 1930s and mid-1950s, unauthorized foreigners who had developed an "equity stake" in the United States could become immigrants under two legalization programs, and 2.7 million migrants, 75 percent of whom were Mexicans, became legal immigrants (table 2.3).

However, employer sanctions failed to discourage the entry or employment of unauthorized workers, since new arrivals could easily buy and present false documents to employers. Legalized migrants moved throughout the United States, and unauthorized Mexicans followed these legal pioneers throughout rural America, changing the face of small towns and cities in agricultural areas. Migrants moved within the United States and directly from Mexico to states other than California, Texas, and Florida. As unemployment fell in the 1990s, special agricultural workers (SAWs) were able to move from seasonal farmwork into farm-related jobs in meat and poultry processing as well as construction and services, accelerating the changing face of agricultural areas. The results of these shifts were apparent in DOL surveys of crop workers: the share of SAWs dropped sharply, while the share of unauthorized workers rose. Since the late 1990s, more than half of U.S. crop workers have been unauthorized (table 2.4).

Table 2.3. Characteristics of Legalization Applicants, 1987–88

Characteristic	LA[a]	SAW[b]
Median age at entry (years)	23	24
15 to 44 years old (%)	80	93
Male (%)	57	82
Married (%)	41	42
From Mexico (%)	70	82
Applied in California (%)	54	52
Total applicants	1,759,705	1,272,143

Source: U.S. Immigration and Naturalization Service (1991, 70–74).

LA = legalization applicants; SAW = special agricultural workers.

[a] Persons filing I-687 legalization applications.

[b] Persons filing I-700 legalization applications. About 80,000 farm workers received legal immigrant status under the pre-1982 legalization program.

Table 2.4. Authorized and Unauthorized Crop Workers, 1989–2002

Year	Authorized (%)	Unauthorized (%)
1989–1990	88	12
1991–1992	76	24
1993–1994	59	41
1995–1996	55	45
1997–1998	49	51
1999–2000	45	55
2001–2002	47	53

Source: Carroll et al. (2005).

SEASONAL FARM LABOR MARKETS

Over the past century, U.S. agriculture has grown and generally prospered, as reflected in expanded production and the rising value of farmland. Families that do not hire any workers operate most U.S. farms, but the largest 10 percent of the 150,000 U.S. farms producing high-value fruits, nut, berries, vegetables and melons, and horticultural specialties (fruit, vegetable, and horticultural [FVH] commodities) account for over 75 percent of FVH sales and employment. Labor availability has not been a constraint on the sector's expansion. In 2002 FVH sales were $42 billion, representing 44 percent of total crop sales.

FVH farmers have been the catalyst for changing the face of rural America, often providing the first U.S. jobs for rural Mexicans. The revolving-door nature of FVH farm labor markets shows how the age-old issue of seasonality is dealt with. Average hourly earnings for private-sector U.S. workers are $16 in 2005, so full-time workers employed 2,000 hours a year earn $32,000. Farmworkers earn about half as much per hour as non-farmworkers and work about half as many hours, so they wind up with a quarter of the annual earnings, about $8,000 a year, which is below the 2005 federal poverty level for an individual ($9,570) (U.S. Department of Health and Human Services 2005).

Most seasonal farmworkers are immigrants from Mexico. DOL's National Agricultural Workers Survey (NAWS) has been interviewing workers employed on crop farms since 1989. The NAWS finds that most agricultural workers are young Mexican-born men with little education who speak only Spanish. Most crop workers do not travel south to north within the United States. Instead, most arrive in one area of the United States from a home in Mexico and stay in that area, sometimes commuting an hour or more each way to the fields because of the difficulty finding temporary housing in many rural areas. Most Mexicans arrive in the United States between the ages of 18 and 25, and most are out of the seasonal farm workforce by age 40 (Carroll et al. 2005).

All labor markets recruit, remunerate or motivate, and retain workers, but the fruit and vegetable agriculture market handles these three Rs in unique ways. For example, farmers rarely place ads in newspapers to recruit workers or send recruiters to high school or college campuses in search of workers. More typical is how one farmer described his recruiting strategy: "when we need X amount of workers, we call up the contractor, and they supply the workers" (Martin 2003, ch. 2).

In seasonal industries such as agriculture that require large numbers of workers for short periods, a central clearinghouse that lists vacancies and available workers could be the most efficient way to match hundreds of thousands of workers with a similar number of jobs each year. Such a clearinghouse, which could be operated by employers, unions (hiring halls), or the tax-supported Employment Service (Employment Development Department in California), could minimize unemployment for workers and uncertainty for farmers. But it does not exist. Instead, agriculture's recruiting system depends largely on bilingual contractors and foremen to recruit and often supervise crews of 20 to 40 workers. This decentralized system almost guarantees simultaneous shortages and surpluses, with farmers complaining of labor shortages even while crews remain idle.[8]

Labor markets also remunerate or motivate workers by paying them hourly or piece rate wages. Farmers tend to pay hourly wages when they want slow and careful work, like pruning trees and grape vines, or when they can easily control the pace of work, as when workers walk behind a conveyor belt and put the broccoli or melons they harvest on the moving machine. Piece rates are common when it is hard to regulate the pace of work, as when workers climb trees to pick apples and are thus often out of sight of supervisors, and when quality is less important, as when workers are picking oranges that will be processed into juice. Piece rate wages minimize the need for employers to screen and monitor workers, since it costs the employer $100 to have 1,000 pounds of table grapes picked at 10 cents a pound whether one fast picker or three slow pickers do the work.

The third key labor market function is retention—identifying and encouraging the best seasonal workers to return the next year. Few farm employers have formal personnel systems to identify the best workers, although livestock and dairy farmers who house their year-round workers sometimes consider their hired hands part of the family. More typical is hiring crews of workers and paying piece rate wages so the composition of the crew does not affect the cost of getting a job completed. A comparison with irrigation may be useful. If water is very cheap, farmers often flood a field to ensure that some water trickles to each tree or vine; if water is expensive, rubber hoses can be laid that drip water and nutrients to each tree or vine. By "flooding" the labor market, farmers can ensure that there will be enough workers available, even though the result may be significant unemployment and underemployment.

3

FARM EMPLOYMENT, IMMIGRATION, AND POVERTY

This chapter provides a statistical analysis of the relationship among farm employment, immigration, and poverty. In the 1960s, rural–urban migration, combined with an expansion in labor-intensive fruit, vegetable, and horticultural crops, created a vacuum at the bottom of the job ladder that put upward pressure on agricultural wages and facilitated farmworker unionization. In this high-wage environment, creating new farm or nonfarm jobs could be expected to reduce poverty. During the 1980s and 1990s, the supply of farmworkers expanded because of immigration, mostly from rural Mexico. Today, over 95 percent of those with fewer than two years of U.S. farmwork experience were born abroad (Carroll et al. 2005), and the farmworkers of the future are growing up outside the United States.

The availability of U.S. farm jobs encourages immigration from rural Mexico, and the availability of Mexican migrants stimulates the expansion of U.S. FVH agriculture. There is a circular relationship between farm employment and immigration, as found in a study based on 1980 and 1990 census data for 66 rural California towns with the highest percentages of workers employed in farm jobs (Taylor, Martin, and Fix 1997). In these farmworker towns, most farmworkers had incomes below the federal poverty level because they had relatively low hourly earnings and worked only seasonally. Nationwide, a similar study found a circular relationship between U.S. farm employment and immigration that reduced poverty in 1980 but increased poverty in 1990 (Martin and Taylor 2003).

This chapter shows that the circular relationship between farm employment and immigration persisted in the 1990s. Testing the hypothesis of a two-way relationship between farm employment and immigration shows that the foreign-born population in the 66 California towns studied by Taylor, Martin, and Fix (1997) continued to rise and that more farm employment was associated with more poverty.

THEORY AND HYPOTHESES

The usual assumption in the United States is that poor people can work their way out of poverty. However, if the jobs they find offer low wages, then having more people in jobs can result in more poverty, not less. Since new farmworkers come from abroad, more farmworker jobs mean more immigration. Foreign-born workers may be willing to migrate to low-paying agricultural jobs in the United States if these jobs pay more than what workers would earn in their country of origin. In turn, the availability of migrants stimulates the creation of new farm jobs, as farmers plant crops expecting there will be workers to harvest them.[1]

Martin and Taylor (2003) found that an additional 100 farm jobs were associated with an average 34-person increase in the foreign-born population in U.S. census tracts, regardless of whether these tracts are largely agricultural or nonagricultural. They also found that a 100-person increase in the foreign-born population in the same census tract increased farm employment slightly, by 0.31 jobs. The effect of immigration on farm employment was small (though statistically significant) because, although nearly all farmworkers were immigrants, most immigrants worked in manufacturing and services, not farm jobs.

Martin and Taylor also found that increases in farm employment reduced poverty in U.S. census tracts in 1980: a 100-person increase in the farm workforce was associated with a 57-person decrease in people living in impoverished households. However, this favorable effect reversed in 1990, when a 100-person increase in farm employment was associated with an 85-person *increase* in poverty. Exactly why more farm jobs were associated with less poverty in the 1980s and more poverty in the 1990s is unknown, but the answer probably lies in the spread of Mexican migrants and seasonal farm jobs throughout the United States, as midwestern and northeastern farms that once had a year-round hired hand became more likely to hire a crew of seasonal workers when they were needed.

This chapter uses profiles of the 66 rural California towns from Martin, Fix, and Taylor (1997), updated with Census 2000 data.[2] Farm employment and immigration, both of which potentially influence poverty, were modeled in as simultaneous outcomes. The statistical analysis controls for employment, immigration, and poverty in the previous census year and addresses the question, "Given immigration, farm employment, and poverty in 1990, what are the key variables explaining the poverty we observe in 2000?" This model corresponds to a structural partial-equilibrium model of farm labor demand, immigrant labor supply, and poverty outcomes and is summarized in the appendix.

The definitions of the three dependent variables follow.

Farm labor demand—the share of employment in farm jobs in each community in 2000. Given high levels of unemployment in rural areas and an elastic or highly responsive supply of immigrant farm labor, farm employment is primarily demand driven, with more workers arriving when they are needed. A key hypothesis of this research is that the relationship between farm employment and migration is circular: farm employment stimulates migration, which stimulates farm employment. To test this simultaneity hypothesis, farm employment was modeled as a function of the share of foreign-born in-town populations, and the farm employment equation also includes as an explanatory variable the share of the workforce in farm jobs in the previous census as a proxy or control for the structure of local labor markets.

Foreign-born population—the share of foreign-born persons in 2000. The foreign-born share of the population is used as a proxy or indicator of the supply of immigrant labor available to farms. Although most foreign-born workers in the 66 sampled California towns are not employed in agriculture, virtually all new entrants into the farm workforce are immigrants. Many variables may influence immigration; the migration model attempts to control for these variables. Hypothetically, farm labor demand is a key variable explaining the foreign-born share of a town's population. It is included in the foreign-born equation to test the hypothesis that farm employment stimulates immigration, creating a circular relationship between farm labor demand and immigration.

An extensive theoretical and empirical literature on the determinants of immigration generally places migration determinants in three groups. The first consists of "push" factors stimulating migration at migrant origins, including variables that affect the opportunity cost of migrating: wages, employment rates, and characteristics of migrant-sending areas (market imperfections) that shape migration and remittance impacts on migrant-source areas. The second group is "pull" factors, such as income and employment prospects, at migrant destinations. The third is migration costs, which depend not only on distance but also on networks of family or friends at migrant destinations who can provide advice and sometimes funds to finance the trip. The immigration equation controls for these variables (insofar as they vary across rural California communities) by including, as an explanatory variable, the foreign-born share in the previous census as well as the town's total population.

Poverty—the share of people in households with incomes below the poverty level. Poverty is hypothesized to be positively related to the share of farm jobs in a community. To test this hypothesis, the share of the population living in poverty is modeled as a function of the share of the workforce employed in farm jobs. If farm employment does not affect poverty, then the relationship between these two variables should equal zero, while a positive coefficient on farm employment would support the hypothesis that farm employment continued to be positively associated with poverty in 2000.

Immigration in response to employment can influence poverty independently, because most immigrants in rural areas are poor. The foreign-born share of the town population is thus included as an explanatory variable in the poverty equation. The determinants of poverty are complex, and the poverty equation includes the number of poor persons in the previous census to act as a proxy for variables influencing poverty at the community level; the labor force participation rate; and dependency ratios, the share of residents younger than 15 and older than 65. Other things being equal, one would expect that the higher the elderly and child populations, the larger the share of people in poverty.

Each of the three equations includes as an explanatory variable the level of the dependent variable observed in the previous census.[3] Such lagged variables are used for two reasons: they are largely exogenous, having been determined at least 10 years earlier, and the unobserved factors shaping them are likely to be similar in 1990 and 2000. These lagged explanatory variables turn out to be highly significant, suggesting a path dependency that makes it hard for an area to change its economy and labor market.

Table 3.1 summarizes the towns and shows that the average town population in 2000 was 7,784 people, 36 percent of which were foreign born. At the time of the census, 27 percent lived in impoverished households and 24 percent were employed in agriculture. Between 1990 and 2000, the foreign-born share of town populations increased from 30 percent to 36 percent, and the share of workers employed in agriculture decreased from 28 percent to 24 percent. Farm employment increased in almost half the towns, by an average of 34 percent, and decreased in the other half by an average of 31 percent (data not shown). Poverty fell slightly, from 28 percent to 27 percent, between 1990 and 2000.

Table 3.1. Census Snapshot of 66 Rural California Towns, 1990 and 2000

	Year	
	1990	2000
Variable	(SD)	(SD)
Average share of population living in poverty[a]	28	27
	(14)	(10)
Average share of population that is foreign born	30	36
	(13)	(13)
Average share of the workforce in farm jobs	28	24
	(16)	(15)
Average town population	5,884	7,784
	(4,297)	(5,749)
Average share of population younger than 15 or older than 65	45	37
	(4)	(4)
Average share of working-age population in workforce	61	58
	(8)	(9)

Sources: 1990 and 2000 U.S. census data.

SD = standard deviation.

Notes: These 66 towns are those in the California Rural Community (CARUCOM) database with populations between 1,000 and 20,000 and with 8 percent or more of their workforces employed principally in agriculture; see http://www.migration.ucdavis.edu/rmn/rural_data/carucom/car ucom.html.

[a]To determine who is in poverty, the Census Bureau uses money income thresholds that vary by family size and composition. If a family's total income is less than the family's threshold, then that family and every individual in it is considered in poverty. The poverty threshold for a family of four in 2000 was $17,603. See http://www.census.gov/hhes/www/poverty/poverty00/thresh00.html.

FARM JOBS, IMMIGRATION, AND POVERTY: A VICIOUS CIRCLE

Table 3.2 confirms the circular relationship between farm employment, immigration, and poverty. A 1 percentage-point increase in the farm share of the workforce was associated with a 0.51 percentage-point increase in the foreign-born population share. A 1 percentage-point increase in foreign-born share, in turn, was associated with a 0.85 percentage-point increase in the share of workforce in agriculture. Meanwhile, a 1 percentage-point increase in the share of the workforce in farm jobs, other things being equal, increased the share of the population in poverty by 0.39 percentage points. However, the share of foreign-born did not significantly affect the poverty rate.

Figure 3.1 compares the 1990–2000 findings with those for the 1980s (the corresponding findings for 1980–90 appear in parentheses). The figure changes percentages to absolute changes in the key variables of interest. Other things being equal, an additional 100 farm jobs increased the foreign-born population by 186 people in 2000, meaning the immigration multiplier of an additional farm job was more than 1.8. A 100-person increase in foreign-born population was associated with a 59-person increase in farm employment, suggesting the availability

Table 3.2. Farm Employment, Immigration, and Poverty Interactions in 66 California Towns, 1990 and 2000

| | EQUATION | | | | | |
| | Poverty | | Farm Employment | | Immigration | |
Variable	Estimated coefficient	t-ratio	Estimated coefficient	t-ratio	Estimated coefficient	t-ratio
	Endogenous					
Share of workforce in farm jobs in 2000	0.39***	4.06			0.51***	5.23
Share of population that is foreign born in 2000	−0.13	−1.19	0.85***	6.46		
	Exogenous					
Share of workforce in farm jobs in 1990			0.00	1.41		
Share of population that is foreign born in 1990					0.01***	5.31
Total population in 2000	<0.01	0.40				
Share of population living in poverty in 1990	0.15**	2.32				
Share of population younger than 15 in 2000	0.87***	3.17				
Share of population older than 65 in 2000	0.01	0.04				
Share of working-age population in workforce in 2000	−0.33**	−2.61			−0.02***	−4.66
Intercept of regression line	0.10	1.38	−0.09**	−2.15	0.24***	8.25

Source: Authors' estimates using 1990 and 2000 census data.

Notes: Numbers in table are estimated effects of a change in the row variable on the column variable. For example, a 0.01 increase in the share of workforce in agriculture is associated with a 0.39×0.01 or 0.39 percentage-point increase in poverty. Blank cells indicate that the (row) variable was included in the (column) equation, based on theoretical considerations and exclusion restrictions required to estimate simultaneous equation models.

*p < .05; ** p < .01; *** p < .001.

Figure 3.1. Farm Employment, Immigration, and Poverty Interactions, 1990–2000

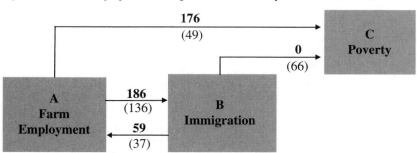

Source: Three-stage least squares estimation of immigration and farm employment equations and ordinary least squares estimation of poverty equation using 1990 and 2000 census data.
Notes: Numbers in parentheses are for 1980–90. All estimates are significant below the .05 level.

of immigrant workers encouraged labor-intensive agriculture to expand. An additional 100 farm jobs were associated with 176 more poor people in 2000, suggesting a poverty multiplier of an additional farm job of just under 1.8, including the farmworker plus an additional 0.8 household members. Immigration contributed to poverty indirectly, by stimulating the creation of new, low-paying farm jobs.

The farm employment–immigration–poverty interaction became more pronounced in the 1990s, since most of the multipliers were larger in 2000 than in 1990. An additional 100 farm jobs were associated with 186 more immigrants in 2000, versus 136 in 1990, and 176 more poor residents in 2000, compared with 49 in 1990. In 1990, controlling for farm employment, immigration directly increased poverty because most of the foreign-born in rural California were poor. In 2000, however, the direct effect of immigration on poverty disappeared, and farm employment, not immigration per se, was the dominant variable explaining poverty.

Several of the control variables are significant and have the expected effects. Rural poverty is persistent: the 2000 poverty rate is significantly and positively related to the poverty rate in 1990. Poverty is significantly higher in towns with a high share of children in the population. All towns had a high share of their workers employed in agriculture in 1990, but several towns experienced rapid growth of nonfarm jobs, which is why the average share of farmworkers dropped over the decade.

Immigration is significantly and positively related to the share of the population that is foreign born in 1990, reflecting migration networks and family unification. Controlling for all other variables, a 1 percentage-point increase in the foreign-born population share in 1990 was associated with a 0.07 percentage-point increase in the foreign-born population in 2000—that is, there were 1.25 foreign-born residents in 2000 for every foreign-born person in the town in 1990.

These data apply to 66 farmworker towns and may not hold generally. These towns are among the poorest in California, and the findings are indicative of the farm employment–immigration–poverty interactions in such communities. High immigration and persistent poverty are a general feature of the San Joaquin Valley, California's agricultural heartland. If the seven San Joaquin Valley counties of Fresno, Kings, Merced, Kern, Madera, Stanislaus, and Tulare were a separate state, it would be the largest farm-state except for California and the 23rd largest state in population. However, this "SJV state" would have the highest unemployment rate, the lowest per capita income, and the highest poverty rate in the United States.

Two Scenarios

These rural farmworker towns are ports of entry for newcomers from rural Mexico. The analysis indicates that farm employment, not immigration, is the primary reason for the towns' high poverty rates, as each additional farm job was associated with a 1.8-person increase in the number of poor people from 1990 to 2000. The association between farm employment and rural poverty became more pronounced in the 1990s, as expanding farm employment attracted new immigrants. In 2000, each additional farm job was associated with a 1.9-person increase in the foreign-born population.

There is a vicious circle of farm employment, immigration, and poverty. The result is a seemingly prosperous agriculture marked by well-kept crops and persistent poverty in nearby farmworker towns. Figure 3.2 compares per capita incomes in the rural communities in which more than 50 percent of residents were foreign born in 2000. It shows that, in 11 of 12, per capita incomes averaged less than $10,000 a year. In eight towns, per capita income was less than the average in Mexico, after adjusting for the lower cost of living in Mexico.[4]

The vicious circle of farm employment, immigration, and poverty raises difficult policy challenges. Low-skilled immigrants and their children have limited prospects for upward mobility in seasonal agriculture as currently structured. The optimistic scenario is that the vicious circle can be reversed; raising worker productivity in some commodities through mechanization or better labor management, as the labor co-ops did in the 1960s and 1970s, could ensure that each worker gets more hours of work. Most rural communities hope that the creation of nonfarm jobs will alleviate poverty and provide jobs for farmworkers' children who reject their parents' jobs in the fields.

Figure 3.2. Per Capita Incomes in the Highest Immigration Rural California Towns, 2000

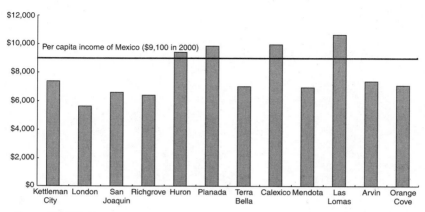

Source: 2000 U.S. Census.

Notes: These towns are the communities in the CARUCOM database in which more than 50 percent of residents were foreign born in 2000. Towns are arranged by percentage of foreign-born from highest (Kettleman City, 62.1%) to lowest (Orange Cove, 50.3%). Mexico per capita income is adjusted for purchasing power parity, which reflects the lower cost of living in Mexico. Average incomes in rural Mexico, from which most California farmworkers originate, are lower than the average for all of Mexico.

The pessimistic scenario is that the vicious circle will intensify as more newcomers arrive from southern Mexico and Central America, where many residents have even less human capital.

PART 2

CHANGING THE FACE OF RURAL AMERICA

The three chapters in this part explore the impacts of immigrants in the inland agricultural valleys of California, the coastal valleys, and the meat and poultry processing centers in Delaware and Iowa. The chapters are based on reports prepared for seminars in these regions. The chapters analyze census, administrative, and other data to paint pictures of how employers came to rely on newcomer migrants, how local leaders perceived the integration of migrants and their children, and how migrants and their children saw their prospects for upward mobility in the United States.

4

CALIFORNIA: INLAND AGRICULTURAL VALLEYS

SAN JOAQUIN VALLEY

The San Joaquin Valley, centered on Fresno, has about 3.5 million residents and an economy based on agriculture. The three southern San Joaquin Valley counties—Fresno, Tulare, and Kern—are the leading farm counties in the United States, and their combined farm sales of almost $10 billion exceed those of more than 40 states. In addition to significant milk and cotton production, the San Joaquin Valley produces most U.S. wine, raisin, and table grapes; most fresh oranges and melons; and most tree fruits, such as plums, peaches, and nectarines. About 500,000 individuals are employed on the Valley's farms sometime during a typical year, with employment peaking in September and unemployment reaching 15 to 20 percent in February.

There has long been poverty in what has been dubbed "the U.S. fruit bowl," and this poverty was the background for *The Grapes of Wrath* in the 1930s and the table grape boycott launched by the UFW in 1966 that was dubbed La Causa. Today, poverty persists and labor paradoxes abound in a much-expanded agriculture. Fresno County, the nation's largest farm county and the county with 6 of the 10 poorest cities in the state, illustrates the importance of agriculture to the local economy. In 2003, an average 46,000 of the 329,000 employed workers were wage workers on farms, and the farm share of total employment matched the unemployment rate, 14 percent. Employment on Fresno

County farms in 2003 peaked at 65,000 in September and reached a trough of 31,000 in February–March.

Raisins

Fresno's raisin industry epitomizes the challenges involved in using immigrant workers to fill seasonal farm jobs. Almost all U.S. raisin grapes are produced on 125,000 to 150,000 acres near Fresno, and harvesting them has been the single most labor-intensive farming activity in North America for most of the past half-century. Each August and September, farmers measure the rising sugar level in their grapes; when it reaches 20 to 24 percent,[1] the 3,500 raisin farmers need 40,000 to 50,000 workers to cut down the bunches of grapes with a sharp knife, collect them in a tub, and lay them on paper trays to dry into raisins.[2] There is a labor shortage every year as farmers wait for sugar levels to rise and then want the grapes picked immediately to maximize the drying time before the mid-September rains hit. About 4.5 pounds of grapes dry into 1 pound of raisins, and the record 400,000 tons of U.S. raisins produced in 2000 were a third of the world's supply; a third of U.S. raisins are typically exported.

How should society weigh the trade-offs in raisin harvesting between farmers who want to maximize the value of their crop and workers who want to maximize seasonal earnings? From a farmer's point of view, having a large seasonal workforce on standby is the best way to ensure that the raisins will be picked and dried at just the right time. However, larger workforces and shorter seasons mean lower wages for workers, who are likely to be unemployed as they wait for harvesting and again after the harvest is completed.

Most farmers believe that the best way to pick raisins in a timely manner is to import guest workers from lower-wage countries who are satisfied to remain on standby until sugar levels are optimal. Workers are paid a piece rate of about $0.01 a pound to harvest the green grapes that dry into raisins, and most earn $8 to $10 an hour. However, even working seven days a week during the six-week harvest, most workers earn less than $3,000, a third of the federal poverty level but more than many workers in rural Mexico earn in a year.

Raisins can be harvested mechanically, provided optimal sugar levels are attained earlier in the season using certain grape varieties. If optimal sugar levels are reached in early August, for example, the canes, each with 10 to 15 bunches of green grapes, can be cut so raisins can begin to dry while they are still on the vine.[3] Once the grapes have partially dried into raisins on the vine, a wine grape harvester with rotating fingers can brush the raisins from the vine, allowing them to fall to a conveyor belt that transports them onto a continuous paper tray as individual raisins, where they finish drying in a few days. In this way, the raisins are ready to be picked up mechanically and taken to a facility to be packaged much earlier than under the traditional hand-harvesting system, minimizing labor requirements as well as the risk of rain damage. Farmers can also train grape vines to grow on trellises that bridge rows, maximizing the leaves exposed to the sun and more than doubling yields—to five tons an acre or more—while allowing fully mechanized dried-on-the-vine raisins to be sold as a natural product that has never touched the ground.[4]

The economics of raisin mechanization are compelling. New vineyards are planted so the grapes can be harvested mechanically, meaning that strong metal stakes anchor the wires or cordons on which grape vines grow. Owners of older vineyards must retrofit them for mechanical harvesting, investing $1,500 to $2,500 an acre to add stronger stakes and new wires. The machines used to harvest partially dried raisin grapes cost $150,000 or more, although smaller raisin growers can use custom harvesters. A grower near retirement producing two tons of raisins worth $800 a ton or $1,600 an acre may decide it is preferable to urge farmers' associations to lobby for a guest worker program and continue to hand-harvest rather than mechanize.

Aging owners of small vineyards who are unsure how long they will remain in business are a major reason the industry has been slow to mechanize. Another reason is that, with plenty of workers available over the past two decades, mechanization has seemed unnecessary. Also, growers like to switch the uses of their grapes in response to prices. Thompson seedless grapes can be harvested as table grapes, wine grapes, or raisin grapes. But the dried-on-the-vine system is designed specifically for raisin grapes, so growers are less able to change how these grapes will be harvested. Ownership patterns, immigration, and flexibility encourage maintaining the raisin harvesting status quo, particularly when trade negotiations could increase competition from Turkey and China, each of which can produce raisins significantly cheaper than the United States can. In 2004, an estimated 70 percent of raisin acres and 80 percent of raisins were picked in the traditional way, with workers hand-cutting bunches of grapes and laying them on paper trays.

Parlier

The impact of the traditional raisin harvesting system is apparent in such cities as Parlier, one of 15 cities in Fresno County. Many local residents and migrant newcomers have never heard of the World Trade Organization and do not understand how easy it is to use wine grape harvesters in raisin vineyards, but they do know that it is becoming harder to find work. With more newcomers eager for jobs, the labor contractors who do most of the hiring can keep wages down.

The 2000 Census reported that Parlier had 11,000 residents. Most adults had very little education: 52 percent did not finish 9th grade, 66 percent did not finish high school, and only 3 percent had college degrees. Most are Spanish speaking: 82 percent of those over 5 years old spoke Spanish at home, making it easier to live in Parlier speaking Spanish than English and explaining why Parlier seems more of a Mexican than a U.S. town. The data do not suggest a bucolic place: theft is common, and iron bars protect many homes and businesses.

Parlier's per capita income was $7,100 in 1999, less than half the average for the county and a third of the U.S. and state averages, but more than the per capita gross national income of Mexico, which was $4,400.[5] Most Parlier residents are farmworkers, and the local job pyramid is very steep. About 62 percent of those age 16 and older were in the labor force in April 2000, when 3,300 were employed and 1,200 were unemployed, an unemployment rate of 27 percent. Of the 4,900 Parlier residents who worked in 1999, a third worked less than 26 weeks, and the 1,300 who worked full time and year round had median earnings of $17,000. Most Parlier residents are poor, but the receipt of welfare benefits is uneven, since many are not eligible for benefits.[6]

Parlier's Hispanics took control of city government in the early 1970s, and the new leaders embraced affordable housing. One-sixth of Parlier's residents receive some form of housing subsidy, making the city one of the largest per capita users of USDA subsidies for rural housing and infrastructure. Parlier welcomes developers, who in 2004 offered entry-level homes for less than $100,000 and "executive homes" that started at $180,000. Available, affordable housing has turned Parlier into a city of farmworkers who commute to nearby fields as well as a growing number of non-farmworkers—often children of farmworkers—who commute to jobs in nearby cities.

Many of the newest farmworkers live in "back houses." Parlier has flexible housing regulations, permitting garage conversions to provide housing for family members but not for unrelated renters, and the local government loosely enforces this rule. Back houses include converted garages as well as sheds in backyards, and they may house half the 4,000 migrants who come to the area each summer. In many cases, newly arrived unauthorized men each pay $30 to $40 a week for a room with six to eight others, food, and rides to work, making the farmworker service economy perhaps 10 percent of the city's economic output. Some observers believe that Parlier's flexible housing policies help minimize tensions between newcomers and established residents, since established residents gain economically from continued immigration.

Parlier also has one of the largest publicly funded migrant farmworker housing centers in the United States, with 130 two- and three-bedroom units for legal families that earn most of their income from farmwork or food processing and have usual homes at least 50 miles away.[7] Over 80 percent of the center's residents are from south Texas, and many are associated with the farmworker service economy as foremen, raiteros (those who drive workers to the fields in their vans for $4 to $5 a day), or cannery and packinghouse workers. As with other migrant centers, the Parlier center is filled soon after it opens in early April; returning residents receive priority to move in and take advantage of on-site, no-cost child care provided by Migrant Head Start and low-cost health care services at a nearby clinic.

Parlier has recently shifted its focus from affordable housing to economic development, partly in response to accusations that previous city leaders associated with the federally funded United Health Centers clinic encouraged construction of affordable housing to maximize the pool of farmworker clients. Parlier tried and failed to attract technology companies and "big box" retailers; in 2004, the city issued a $7 million bond to attract biomass and biotech companies to a 300-acre industrial park. Parlier also looks to the state and federal governments for assistance, partnering with nearby farmworker cities in a quest for authority to provide tax breaks to relocating businesses that bring jobs.

Parlier schools are the city's largest employer, with 400 employees, or an eighth of those employed. School board elections are hotly contested, in part because the board controls contracts for maintenance and facilities. However, student performance lags: 40 percent of teens do not finish high school,[8] and those who do stay in school have some of the lowest test scores in the state. Virtually all students qualify for free meals, and 64 percent are classified as English learners. Even though spending per pupil was $7,300 in 2002–03, many teachers say resources are insufficient to take students who do not speak English or have educated parents and prepare them for good U.S. jobs. Many of Parlier's teachers do not live in Parlier.

Local youth seem unanimous in what they do not want to do—work in the fields—but are vague about what they do want to do. Answers range from "making money somehow" to becoming mechanics or equipment operators. On the other hand, several graduates each year go to Ivy League colleges, the result of a teacher taking the best students on a trip east. Many other local youth would like to attend local community colleges or state universities, and most of those who attend college reject careers in agriculture, associating the dominant local industry with the hard work and low wages their parents and relatives experienced.

Over the past century, labor has not been a constraint on the agricultural economy of Fresno County because of the influx of workers to cities such as Parlier. A steady stream of newcomers has created a farmworker service economy in Parlier that has provided jobs for older ex-farmworkers and the U.S.-educated children of farmworkers. Despite some of the lowest incomes and highest unemployment rates in the state, Parlier's population is one of the fastest growing, up 5 percent a year as rural Mexicans continue to see more opportunity in rural California than at home.

The questions are, what will happen to these immigrants when they leave the fields, and what does the future hold for their children who want to avoid going into the fields? Will ex-farmworkers and their children find nonfarm jobs in the construction industry and in the city's new industrial park, thereby achieving the upward mobility of previous immigrants? Or will they wind up in the farmworker service economy, dependent like traditional raisin growers on a continued influx of newcomers? Or will economic mobility in rural America continue to require geographic mobility, as Parlier's poor move to larger cities that offer more opportunity?

Other Parliers

Parlier is not the only crystal ball through which to see the future of an area being populated by migrants from rural Mexico. Other farmworker cities have similar characteristics: increasing populations despite high unemployment rates, few jobs that offer wages sufficient to support middle-class lifestyles, and economic development plans that depend on tax breaks or prisons. These cities face a growing air pollution problem: the 25,000-square-mile San Joaquin Valley violated the eight-hour smog standard 240 times in 2004, the most days of violation in the United States. These violations help explain why 10 percent of residents have chronic breathing disorders.[9]

Huron is a nearby farmworker city. It has been described as "knife-fight city" because of the evening activities of some migrants who descend every spring and fall to cut lettuce. Huron has six bars, five gangs, and a famous drug alley.[10] The city's population is 5,800, and 39 percent of Huron's residents have incomes below the poverty level. Unemployment averages more than 15 percent, and per capita income is among the lowest in the state. Huron aggressively seeks federal grants and received a $3.4 million grant in 1999 to upgrade its water treatment plant, which aided its bids for federal, state, and private prisons to create local jobs.[11] However, very few Huron residents decide Huron's priorities. With children and noncitizens accounting for many of the city's residents, fewer than 10 percent of residents typically vote.

Orange Cove is a farmworker city of 9,000, where many of the adult residents pick or pack oranges. Unemployment averages 30 percent, and more than 40 percent of residents are considered poor. The town has no traffic signals, movie theaters, or major retail shopping centers.[12] The Department of Housing and Urban Development has designated Orange Cove a renewal community, which means that employers hiring additional workers can receive tax credits of up to $1,500 a worker and up to $2,400 for a worker hired from groups with traditionally high unemployment rates or other special needs. Orange Cove donated 60 acres of land in 1999 to Fresno-based La Tapatia Tortilleria, which promised to expand employment from 139 to 239 after moving to Orange Cove.[13]

The rural poverty challenge in Parlier and other farmworker cities echoes across Fresno County, which had 826,000 residents in 2003 and provided at least one of the three major means-tested benefits— CalWORKS, food stamps, and Medi-Cal[14]—to a quarter of its residents. The average cash grant was $635 for 2.2 people, and recipients were 66 percent Hispanic, 14 percent white, and 11 percent Southeast Asian.[15] Fresno County's economic development goal is to create nonfarm jobs related to farming, in such areas as irrigation technologies, that offer wages high enough to allow middle-class lifestyles. The concrete goal is 30,000 additional jobs paying at least $30,000 a year; if accomplished, this goal would reduce Fresno County's unemployment rate from twice the state rate to the state rate.

The challenge involved in creating more high-wage jobs is significant: 60 percent of the unemployed workers requesting unemployment insurance (UI) benefits in Fresno County do not have high school diplomas. One local farmer said, "We've done more for the employment of unskilled individuals than anyone else. . . . Look at the dropout rates in schools and thank God we're out here" to provide farm jobs.[16] Farmworkers generated about 35 percent of the 90,000 UI claims in Fresno County in 2002, and Hispanics, who dominate the farm workforce, accounted for 70 percent of the UI claims (Hispanics are 44 percent of Fresno County residents). Farmers assert that many of the UI claimants also work for cash wages in agriculture, although state officials have not found significant fraud.

In a reversal of 1930s Dust Bowl migration, More Opportunity for Viable Employment (MOVE), a local community organization, has subsidized the relocation of welfare recipients to the Midwest since 1998. Meatpackers have made recruiting trips to the San Joaquin Valley, knowing that San Joaquin Valley welfare recipients can receive relocation assistance grants of $300 to $1,600 in exchange for staying away from the San Joaquin Valley for at least 180 days. In addition to these departure bonuses, some meatpackers offer non–welfare recipients bus tickets to the Midwest and interest-free loans or cash advances to obtain housing. Reports in 2001–02 suggested that 85 percent of those who received assistance to leave the San Joaquin Valley stayed away at least six months.[17]

SACRAMENTO VALLEY

The Sacramento Valley, which extends from the state capital in Sacramento to Redding in the north, has an economy anchored in the shrinking agriculture and timber industries. Most residents are non-Hispanic whites who complain that the area exports farm commodities, timber, and young people. Asian and Hispanic immigrants are moving to the Sacramento Valley in search of seasonal farm jobs and low-cost housing. The challenge is to help these newcomers, who lack education but have (in the eyes of many employers) a good work ethic, move up the job ladder while also assisting local residents, who have more education but are perceived to lack good work attitudes.

The shrinking economic base in the Sacramento Valley has generated welfare and unemployment indicators that are among the highest in the state. Two counties illustrate the economic challenge. Yuba County often leads the state in the percentage of residents receiving cash assistance, while nearby Colusa County often has the state's highest unemployment rate. However, what makes the Sacramento Valley an interesting contrast to the San Joaquin Valley is that there is widespread poverty despite a largely mechanized agriculture and relatively little immigration.

Sutter–Yuba

Sutter (77,000 residents in 2000, according to the Census) and Yuba (60,000 residents in 2000) counties are in the southern end of the Sacramento Valley, near but not part of the Interstate 80 corridor that connects Sacramento to the Bay Area and Reno. The two major cities, Yuba City (in Sutter County), with 35,000 residents, and Marysville (in Yuba County), with 13,000, face each other across the Feather River, with Yuba City considered the growth node for the area.

Yuba is the poorer of the two counties, with only two incorporated cities and poorer farmland, some of which was subdivided in the 1930s and settled by small farmers from the Midwest whose descendants, as well as Hmong migrants who moved to the area for its low-cost housing, are concentrated. The federal government owns much of the county's land, giving Yuba a relatively small tax base (the largest employer is Beale Air Force Base). Much of Yuba County is in a floodplain, which limits the growth of the county seat in Marysville: it is surrounded on all sides by levees.

In 1990, the population of Sutter and Yuba counties was 73 percent white and 13 percent Hispanic, and there were more Asian Indians (4,600) than either blacks (3,400) or Native Americans (2,600), according to the 1990 Census. The area's population is changing, with the Asian and Hispanic share rising rapidly—Spanish, Hmong, and Punjabi are the major first languages of limited English proficient students. Relatively few children prepare for or go on to higher education: only 33 percent of Yuba County graduates planned to attend college in 1999, versus 60 percent statewide.[18] Some local employers complain that local high school graduates do not have appropriate work attitudes; as a result, employers prefer Hispanic immigrants who may lack a high school education but who work harder.

The Sutter–Yuba metropolitan statistical area (both counties combined) had an average labor force of 57,600 in 1998 and an average unemployment rate of 14.5 percent; unemployment varied from 9.7 percent in September to 19.4 percent in February. There were 44,000 persons on payrolls in Yuba and Sutter counties in June 1999, including almost 8,000 (18 percent) employed on farms, 11,000 employed by government, 9,000 employed in trade, and 3,000 employed in manufacturing. Training programs find that the hardest persons to retrain are men who previously had high-wage jobs in the timber industry, since they must retrain for lower-wage jobs. Their homemaker wives who are entering or reentering the labor market have been far more willing to learn new skills.

The share of the workforce employed in agriculture closely tracks shares of foreign-born residents. Colusa County, just west of Sutter County, has the largest share of foreign-born residents in the area and the highest percentage of workers in farm jobs (28 percent). Colusa County is the leading U.S. rice producer and produces the processing tomatoes used to make ketchup. Rice is a low-value, water-intensive crop grown in clay soil that minimizes seepage of water away from plants; the land on which it is planted probably would not be farmed if it were not used to grow rice.

Yuba County, with the smallest share of foreign-born residents in the region, has the smallest percentage of workers employed in agriculture (8 percent), with Sutter County at 11 percent. Yuba County vies with Merced County for the highest percentage of residents on welfare; about 14 percent of residents in each county received cash assistance (Temporary Assistance for Needy Families [TANF]) in 1998.[19] The fact that most welfare recipients in Yuba and Sutter counties are non-Hispanic whites has led to speculation that welfare recipients move to the area for lower costs of living, especially if they were originally from the area.[20]

Peaches are the major labor-intensive crop grown in Sutter and Yuba counties, typically providing about 40 percent of the state's peaches.

Machines pick some 30 to 40 percent of the peaches, at a cost of $15 a ton; workers pick the other 60 to 70 percent by hand, at a cost of $30 a ton. Canneries, which pay about $200 a ton for the peaches grown in the area that are processed, pay $15 to $50 a ton less for machine-picked peaches.[21] Hourly labor costs in 1998 were $7 to $8 for skilled labor (e.g., tractor drivers) and $5.75 (the state's minimum wage) to $6 for unskilled labor.

Housing and Hope

Housing for farmworkers is scarce because periodic floods destroy low-cost and temporary housing. Many farmworkers live in old motels or houses, three or four to a room for $1 to $8 a night. Federal, state, and local governments have built housing, but advocates say there is never enough, especially for newcomers to the farm labor force. For example, after the January 1997 floods, the Federal Emergency Management Agency said farmworker housing should be a grower business expense and refused to provide federal dollars to build emergency housing for migrants who arrived the following summer to work. In summer 1999, new two-bedroom family units costing $7.50 a day with easy access to no-cost child care were vacant; advocates attributed the vacancy rates to the cost and the requirement that residents be in the United States legally.[22]

Hope for economic development rests on two foundations: becoming a bedroom community for the Sacramento area, about an hour south, which could stimulate local construction and service industries, and developing a racetrack and concert site to draw visitors to the area. A 20,000-seat Bill Graham Presents amphitheater opened in 2000, followed by the Yuba County Motorplex. However, business development officials say that the nonfarm workforce, largely non-Hispanic whites, are "uneducated, unemployed or underemployed, often drug- and welfare-dependent and suffer from a variety of other social troubles."[23] A local workforce survey of employers found that the top three qualities they were seeking in job applicants were a good work ethic, no drugs, and a clean appearance.[24]

It is hard to overcome perceptions that the Sutter–Yuba area is an undesirable place to live, since it has been wracked by "devastating floods, occasional high-profile crimes, chronic unemployment and, at best, limited cultural amenities" in the words of the *Wall Street Journal*.[25] The 1999 *Places Rated Almanac* ranked Sutter–Yuba 352nd of 354 listed metropolitan areas in the United States and Canada, ahead of Vineland–Millville–Bridgeton, New Jersey, and Kankakee, Illinois. Sutter–Yuba faces two potential threats: the closure of the air force base and water marketing, which could reduce the acreage planted to rice if farmers send their water to Southern California.

IMPERIAL VALLEY

The Imperial Valley is unique among California's inland agricultural regions because it shares a border with Mexico and is largely isolated from the rest of California. Imperial Valley agriculture has closer ties to neighboring Arizona than to the San Joaquin Valley. Imperial County is flanked by Mexicali,[26] the capital of Baja California, to the south; the Salton Sea, a large and shallow sea receiving drainage water from Imperial Valley farmland, to the north; San Diego to the west; and the Colorado River and Arizona to the east. Calexico is the U.S. port of entry for Mexicans who commute to Imperial, and the much larger city of Mexicali across the border is the potential economic engine of the region.

Imperial County faces significant challenges that arise from seasonal farmwork, slow employment growth, and low wages. The Imperial Valley is hot and arid, receiving only three inches of rain a year, and has been described as a 100-mile-long trench with 600,000 acres of farmland below sea level. The key to its agricultural success is low-priced water from the Colorado River, which was brought to the area in 1900 by the California Land Company; nonirrigated land in the area is desert.[27] The Imperial Valley tilts south to north, so irrigation water is delivered from the All-American Canal on the border with Mexico to Imperial farmland by gravity.

Desert Agriculture

Imperial Valley farmland is worth very little without water. However, the farmland was worth almost $2 billion in 2000, when the county had farm sales of $1 billion. The area has three major agricultural sectors: field crops, livestock, and vegetables and melons. Over half the irrigated crop land is used either to grow field crops such as alfalfa and grasses,[28] wheat, and cotton, or as pasture for beef cattle and lambs. Another 100,000 to 125,000 acres of land are planted in vegetables and melons, including lettuce and carrots, along with important seed crops.

The two major industries in Imperial County are agriculture and government. In 1999, farm employment was 28 percent of total employment, while government accounted for 27 percent. The largest employers in the county are government agencies, including the Imperial Irrigation District, a state prison in Calipatria, and the El Centro Naval Air Facility, as well as two agribusinesses—crop farmer Jack Brothers

& McBurney Inc. in Brawley and labor contractor L & S Harvesting in El Centro. Recently, government employment has been rising and farm employment has been falling.

Imperial County is unusual because industry or payroll employment (reported by employers) is larger than civilian employment (from the Current Population Survey of households). In September 2000, employer-reported employment was 53,000, versus 43,500 according to the household survey. This discrepancy occurs because some workers employed in Imperial County live in Mexicali, and workers living in Mexicali are included in employer reports but not in the household survey.[29]

Imperial County employment in September 2000 included 15,000 wage and salary workers in agriculture, 13,000 in state and local government, and 8,000 in retail trade.[30] Imperial County farm employment mirrors statewide trends, in the sense that farm production employment is falling and farm services employment is rising, reflecting the shift to hire workers via labor contractors.[31] Employment and unemployment fluctuate seasonally, primarily in response to agriculture and "snowbird tourists," residents of cold-weather states moving into the area, many in mobile homes. In 1999, county unemployment peaked in July–September at 27 percent and reached 19 to 21 percent between December and March. Unemployment was 21 to 22 percent again in May–June.[32]

In 1995, when the federal poverty level for a family of four was $15,569, Imperial County had the state's highest poverty rate—31 percent of its residents lived below the poverty level, compared with 16 percent of all Californians. Imperial County reduced the number of welfare cases from 8,000 in the early 1990s to 4,000 by 2000, primarily as adults were dropped from the rolls. The percentage of children receiving cash assistance has increased as adults have given up the $120 adult share of the typical $620 a month grant for a mother with two children.[33]

Most of the 15,000 to 18,000 seasonal farmworkers employed during the peak January–February season live in Mexicali and commute daily to Imperial Valley farm jobs. Farm labor contractors recruit these commuter workers at the port of entry early each day and take workers to the fields in buses between 5:00 AM and 6:00 AM. Most harvest workers are paid hourly wages close to the 2001 California minimum wage of $6.25 an hour, but some employers pay $0.50 to $1.00 an hour more, especially for more difficult jobs, such as harvesting cauliflower. Most equipment operators, irrigators, and other regular or year-round workers employed on Imperial Valley farms live in the United States, earn more than the minimum wage, and own homes in one of the lowest-cost housing markets in the state.

With the exception of Dole's Bud operations, which have a contract with Teamsters Local 890, few farmworkers are employed under union contracts, although the Imperial Valley was a hotbed of union activity in the late 1920s and the late 1970s. One of the first significant strikes called by Mexican farmworkers in California occurred in 1928, when the Confederation of Mexican Labor Unions organized a strike by melon harvesters to demand higher wages and an end to the requirement that workers be hired via labor contractors. Although no contract was signed, the strike ended when growers agreed to stop withholding 25 percent of each worker's wages until the harvest was completed, and growers rather than labor contractors became responsible for assuring that workers received their full wages.

The UFW's Waterloo

The Imperial Valley loomed large again in 1979, when the first wave of UFW contracts signed under the 1975 Agricultural Labor Relations Act expired. On January 5, 1979, the UFW submitted its economic demands for new contracts to growers and published them in a Mexicali newspaper, *La Voz*. The demands included a 42 percent wage increase for field-workers, bringing the entry hourly wage from $3.70 to $5.25; five more paid holidays; and increased standby and reporting pay for workers. The growers rejected these demands, citing President Carter's recommendation that wages not increase more than 7 percent to avoid adding to inflationary pressures (Martin 2003, ch. 3).

The UFW called a strike involving 4,300 workers by February 1979. There was a great deal of violence and property destruction, as strikers attempted to intimidate strike breakers and flood fields by sabotaging irrigation canals. Growers hired replacement workers as well as security guards, and a foreman killed a UFW striker. In a sign of the tensions, Governor Jerry Brown marched in the funeral procession while local authorities ruled that there was insufficient evidence to prosecute the foreman who fired the fatal shot (Martin 2003, ch. 3).

The strike was settled in 1980 with some growers agreeing to the UFW's wage demands, and the UFW thought that it had won back wages for striking workers from the other growers when the state's Agricultural Labor Relations Board ruled that the growers that did not sign new contracts had failed to bargain in good faith. However, the UFW won a Pyrrhic victory, as many of the growers that signed new contracts with wage increases went out of business and a state appeals court overturned the Agricultural Labor Relations Board's decision, so holdout farmers did not have to pay any back wages. The strike boomeranged on the UFW and raised grower revenues. The supply of winter lettuce decreased by a third in February 1979, but this reduced supply raised grower revenues because lettuce prices tripled; growers had revenue of $69 million in the strike-torn month rather than the usual $39 million (Carter et al. 1981). The labor troubles in Imperial encouraged some growers to shift their winter vegetable production to Arizona.

Despite high unemployment, Imperial County farmers during the 1990s reported farm labor shortages. Three major factors help to explain this apparent paradox. First, the unemployment numbers may be artificially high. Farmworkers employed in Imperial County who live in Mexicali add to Imperial County employment when they are working and some add to Imperial County unemployment when they are jobless, since they can draw UI benefits if they register as available for work. Farm employers say that many UI benefit recipients draw UI benefits under one Social Security number while working for cash wages under another. Second, farm wages have fallen, making farmwork a last resort for workers who may be able to find other jobs.[34] Third, both farm and nonfarm employers are quick to lay off workers when they are not needed; with few other jobs in the area, these employers assume that unemployed workers will be available for work when they are needed.

As agriculture shrinks in the Imperial Valley, local leaders hope that nonfarm private and government jobs can take up the slack. The preferred economic development strategy of local leaders rests on new value-added jobs linked to agriculture, such as a packaged salad plant or a cattle slaughtering facility. However, the area has been most successful attracting prisons, which provide many jobs because of their 24/7 operation. Unfortunately, many local residents do not qualify for prison jobs because they do not have a high school diploma or cannot pass a drug test.

5

CALIFORNIA: COASTAL AGRICULTURAL VALLEYS

NAPA VALLEY

Napa is one of the smallest but best known of California's 58 counties, with 132,000 residents according to the 2000 Census and a projected 158,000 by 2020. Napa is home to world-famous wineries, luxury hotels, and expensive housing developments. But many Hispanics, who are a quarter of its residents, face enormous difficulties finding housing in this affluent area.

Napa County had 555 wine grape growers and 37,500 acres of wine grapes in 1998; its 230 wineries crushed 102,400 tons of grapes, producing about 6.4 million cases of wine. Napa draws an estimated 5 million visitors a year and exemplifies what has been called agri-tourism, turning the production and marketing of farm products into a tourist activity. Unlike seasonal Christmas tree farms or fruit harvesting types of agri-tourism, Napa's wine business has a year-round appeal.[1]

Wine and Wineries

There has been commercial production of wine grapes in California since the 1830s, before California became a state, but phylloxera in the 1870s and Prohibition between 1920 and 1933 almost wiped out the wine grape industry. Wine grapes have become a major agricultural commodity, with almost 3 million tons crushed each year. Worth

$1.5 billion to $2 billion a year, wine grapes represent about half of California's grape production by volume and two-thirds by value.

California had 424,000 acres of wine grapes in 1999. Most of California's wine grapes are grown in the Central Valley, where flat land, yields of 7 to 10 tons an acre, and large acreages encourage mechanical harvesting. Napa produces only 3 percent of California's grapes, but Napa's are the highest-value grapes in the state. In 2000, the best cabernet sauvignon grapes in Napa sold for $3,000 a ton, while Central Valley grapes sold for as little as $125 a ton. Napa's total farm sales were $237 million in 1997, and 96 percent of these sales were wine grapes.

Grape vines grow out of tubes and are trained to grow on cordon wires and begin producing bunches of grapes by the second year. Wine grapes require significant amounts of labor for pruning and harvesting, and the need for hand labor has been increasing as Napa growers shift to higher density plantings and continue to prune and harvest by hand. Pruning to remove last season's cane growth is done between December and February, and harvesting begins in August, when crews of 10 to 20 workers cut bunches of grapes, put them into plastic tubs that hold about 50 pounds, and dump the tubs into gondolas that hold two tons of grapes. Hand harvesting costs $150 to $200 a ton or perhaps $525 for an acre if the yield is three tons. Mechanical harvesting is cheaper, $200 to $300 an acre, but in Napa County, about 75 percent of the grapes are handpicked, reflecting the general rule that more expensive grapes are harvested by hand.[2]

Napa County's labor force averaged 63,100 in 1999, and the unemployment rate averaged 3.3 percent, below the state average. Less than 8 percent of Napa County's employment is in agriculture, compared with 18 percent in Fresno County;[3] food manufacturing (mostly wineries) employed another 10 percent (5,800) of Napa workers.[4] Most of Napa's job growth has been in the service sector, which allows migrants to switch from farmwork to hotels and restaurants and provides nonfarm job opportunities for the children of farmworkers.

Workers may be hired directly by farms or obtained through agricultural service providers (contractors). According to California Employment Development Department data, in 1998 the number of directly hired farmworkers in Napa County peaked at 4,700 in September; the number of agricultural service workers peaked at 1,900 in the same month. The number of directly hired workers hit a low of 2,300 in December, for a peak–trough ratio of 2—that is, two workers were employed in September for every one employed in December. Agricultural services have a higher peak–trough ratio of 3.2, with a low of 600 hires in December.

Housing in Wine Country

The 3,700-person gap between the 6,600 farmworkers employed in September and the 2,900 employed in December leads, among other things, to workers sleeping on church porches in St. Helena and along the Napa River. The visible presence of homeless Mexicans led to fears that this homelessness could hurt agri-tourism. To provide temporary housing for solo male migrants, the Napa Valley Housing Authority in 2001 offered 200 beds in four camps[5] and charged migrants less than the cost of providing room and board, about $11.50 a day versus the actual cost of $18 a day.[6] Wine grape growers who do not provide housing for their workers paid $8.49 per acre of crop-producing land in 2001 to help cover the deficits of the camps.

Despite these efforts, migrants still sleep along the Napa River and seek jobs in grocery store parking lots, and their presence has led to considerable debate about farmworker housing. Most seasonal workers in Napa live in normal housing and apartments like non-farmworkers, and many commute to Napa jobs from lower-cost areas outside Napa Valley, just as many non-farmworkers do. The county and its wine industry are debating ways to close the gap between the demand for and supply of temporary farmworker housing. There are several options, including mechanization, more temporary housing, and more commuting.

Most California grapes are harvested mechanically. If more Napa grapes were picked mechanically, there would be less need for migrant harvest workers and less need for temporary housing. However, wineries have gained the upper hand in dictating grape growing practices, and they argue that premium wines require hand-picked grapes.

The second option would be to build more subsidized temporary farmworker housing. Napa land is very expensive, and a county ordinance requires a minimum of 20 acres to construct temporary farmworker housing and 40 acres to construct year-round farmworker housing. Those who want to preserve Napa say that relaxing this rule would unleash development, although Napa voters in 2002 approved Measure L to allow the construction of migrant farmworker housing for up to 12 workers on land zoned for agriculture outside the county's five cities.[7]

Another option is commuting. Napa is surrounded by lower-cost areas, and employers or the county could subsidize commuting from these lower-cost areas.

Napa is well known among farmworkers for having some of the highest farm wages in the state, often $12 to $15 an hour. However, workers also know that housing is expensive and that hours of farmwork may be limited, since many wineries want grapes picked only in the morning. The dilemma for employers and the county is how to provide housing for very seasonal workers who are likely to combine farm and nonfarm work. Napa growers have played a prominent role in seeking solutions to the lack of affordable housing for farmworkers, but they have also been strong proponents of efforts to limit population growth and to keep much of the county's land zoned for agricultural use. As a result, housing remains expensive and often out of reach for very seasonal workers.

For many farmworkers, Napa is "as good as it gets" because hourly wages are among the highest in the state, and some workers find employment for 8 to 12 months a year. A significant number of workers commute between homes in Mexico and long-season jobs in Napa,[8] and some own houses in both places or their seniority permits them to return to the best temporary housing in Napa. The children of farmworkers, educated in the United States, find various nonfarm jobs in Napa's fast-growing tourism industry.

SALINAS VALLEY

Since the 1920s, Monterey County has been the "Salad Bowl of the World," known for the production of iceberg lettuce and other vegetables. John Steinbeck, the only person to win both the Nobel and Pulitzer prizes for literature, grew up in the Salinas Valley and worked in its sugar beet fields in the 1930s before moving to Carmel, where he did much of his writing.

Salad Bowl Farming

Monterey County agriculture is unique for its emphasis on the production of high-value fresh vegetables and is known for innovations that range from vacuum-cooling lettuce to packaging salads. Salinas Valley farmers were in the forefront of efforts to introduce modern personnel management, hiring even seasonal workers in a central location, using written applications, developing company handbooks that laid out work rules, and training supervisors to treat workers fairly. Many of the largest integrated grower-packer-shipper firms screened new hires to ensure that they were authorized to work in the United States before the law required it, and local farming leaders predicted that Salinas Valley would stay on the high-wage, legal worker, and direct-hire course set during union activities of the 1970s after immigration reform in 1986.

Reality turned out differently. During the 1990s, farmworker wages fell toward the minimum wage, and some of the largest farm employers went out of business or became strictly nonfarm employers that bought vegetables from independent growers who produced according to their specifications. There was a sharp contrast between the increased concentration of packing and marketing and the decentralization of the farm labor market, and most of Salinas Valley's farmwork was soon performed by workers brought to farms by a variety of middlemen, mostly farm labor contractors.

Salinas farm production and employment expanded as strawberry production increased at the north end of the county and wine grape production rose in the south end. Meanwhile, nearby Santa Clara County experienced the dot-com boom in the late 1990s, sharply increasing employment, incomes, and housing prices and encouraging some Silicon Valley workers to move to northern Monterey County. As Silicon Valley moved south, the question was whether Salinas agriculture, wedged between the booming Monterey peninsula and tourism and high-tech Silicon Valley, could remain attractive to farmworkers.

Integration in Salinas

According to the 2000 Census, Monterey County's 402,000 residents were 47 percent Latino (86 percent of Mexican origin)[9] and 40 percent of Monterey County residents spoke Spanish at home. The county's evolution highlights the hourglass- or barbell-shaped skill distribution in the labor force characteristic of current immigration patterns. The county added people at the top and bottom of the job-skill ladder during the 1990s, as Silicon Valley employees moved to the northern part of the county in search of lower-cost housing and farmworkers entered cities in the southern part of the county to fill farm jobs. This hourglass distribution is evident in educational attainment. The share of adults with at least a bachelor's degree rose from 21 to 25 percent between 1990 and 2000, while the share of adults without a high school diploma also rose, from 27 to 29 percent.

Almost 40 percent of the county's residents, 151,000 people, live in the city of Salinas. The importance of farmworkers is reflected in the fact that Salinas had the highest ratio of males to females among major U.S. cities (with populations of at least 100,000) in 2000—114 to 100. The city of Salinas gained another distinction in 2004–05 when the city council voted to close the library system to save money. Although private funds eventually allowed the John Steinbeck Library and its affiliates to remain open, Salinas almost became the largest U.S. city without a public library.

The Salinas area has some of the most crowded housing in agricultural areas. Some eastern areas of the city with mostly single-story homes have Manhattan-style population densities, reflecting garage conversions and sheds in backyards to house new arrivals from Mexico. The average number of persons per household in the city rose from 3.4 in 1990 to 3.6 in 2000.

Overcrowding is also a problem in the smaller farmworker cities. The mayor of Greenfield, a Salinas Valley city of 13,000, said that even if the housing stock were increased two or three times, new arrivals would still be living in garages. Greenfield is 85 percent Latino, and some parents have complained about Mexican day laborers, who spoke Triqui rather than Spanish, harassing female students going to and from the local high school. In response to the complaints, the INS on April 9, 2001, raided the parking lot where farmworkers waited for jobs and apprehended 39 unauthorized Mexicans. Some activists decried the INS raid, and the city council voted 3–2 in May 2001 for a resolution asking the INS to notify the city at least 72 hours before future raids.

Agriculture is a major industry in Monterey County, and farm-related employment is remarkably stable. Since 1983, employment on farms averaged 22 percent of the county's employment, and farm services (workers employed by custom harvesters and labor contractors) accounted for an average of 56 percent of the county's farm employment.[10] The largest employers include Arroyo Labor Contracting Services, Bud of California, D'Arrigo Brothers Co., Foothill Packing Inc., Norcal Harvesting, Premium Harvesting & Packing, and Quality Farm Labor.

The California Employment Development Department obtains employment data from quarterly employer reports submitted with tax payments. Between 1985 and 2000, farm employment statewide increased by 22 percent, less than the 34 percent expansion of employment in all industries (table 5.1). However, farm employment increased 52 percent in Monterey County, faster than nonfarm employment.

Employers report their employment by month, which allows examination of the seasonality of farm employment. In Monterey County, farm employment peaked in October in 1993 and July in 2001 (table 5.2). Farm services employment became more seasonal between 1993 and 2001, as the ratio of the peak month divided by the trough month rose from 2.3 to 2.5. This seasonality helps to explain why the unemployment rate averaged 11 percent in the 1990s and was 14.5 percent in December 2002. Farmworker cities such as Soledad and Gonzales had the highest unemployment rates, 30–31 percent; Salinas had a 19 percent unemployment rate and the Monterey peninsula an 8 percent rate.

In the mid-1990s, the UFW renewed its organizing activities in the Salinas Valley, settling long-running disputes and launching an effort to organize the fast-growing strawberry workforce. In May 1996, the

Table 5.1. Average Annual Employment, Central California Coast Counties and California, 1985–2000

	1985	1990	1995	2000	1985–2000 change (%)	1995–2000 change (%)
Monterey County						
Employment, all industries	122,800	138,900	141,200	166,400	36	18
Employment, farm (share)	24,200 (20%)	28,500 (21%)	31,900 (23%)	36,900 (22%)	52	16
Production	—	—	13,700	16,400		20
Services	—	—	18,200	20,500		13
Santa Cruz County						
Employment, all industries	76,300	94,900	97,700	105,600	38	8
Employment, farm (share)	7,000 (9%)	10,800 (11%)	11,700 (12%)	8,300 (8%)	19	−29
San Benito County						
Employment, all industries	9,100	11,150	11,970	14,940	64	25
Employment, farm (share)	2,590 (28%)	2,820 (25%)	2,490 (21%)	1,920 (13%)	−26	−23
Santa Clara County						
Employment, all industries	770,900	819,500	836,400	1,035,000	34	24
Employment, farm (share)	4,700 (1%)	4,900 (1%)	4,500 (1%)	5,000 (0%)		11
Production	—	—	3,800	4,000		5
Services	—	—	700	1,000		43
California						
Employment, all industries	11,105,200	12,863,400	12,795,700	14,896,600	34	16
Employment, farm (share)	335,400 (3%)	342,000 (3%)	373,500 (3%)	408,500 (3%)	22	9
Production	232,700	218,200	228,400	228,600	−2	0
Services	102,700	123,800	145,100	179,900	75	24

Source: California Employment Development Department. http://www.calmis.ca.gov/htmlfile/subject/indtable.htm.
— = not available.
Note: Farm production and services data are not available for Santa Cruz and San Benito counties.

Table 5.2. Agricultural Employment by Month: Monterey County, 1993 and 2001

	1993		2001	
	Production	Services	Production	Services
January	7,900	9,200	9,300	11,400
February	8,500	9,800	9,800	11,800
March	10,100	11,900	11,500	15,300
April	14,900	17,600	16,100	22,900
May	17,500	19,500	19,800	26,300
June	18,700	19,500	21,400	25,400
July	18,000	18,700	21,900	28,400
August	18,400	18,600	21,500	27,400
September	18,900	19,300	21,700	27,100
October	18,000	20,900	20,300	25,000
November	14,800	20,400	17,100	22,700
December	10,200	16,400	12,400	16,200
Peak–trough ratio	2.4	2.3	2.4	2.5

Source: California Employment Development Department. http://www.calmis.ca.gov/htmlfile/subject/indtable.htm.

UFW signed a five-year collective bargaining agreement covering 450 BCI workers. BCI was the third-largest U.S. lettuce producer that UFW had boycotted for 17 years. Worker advocates heralded the agreement as a new beginning, since the original UFW protagonists, Cesar Chavez and Ted Taylor, had since died. However, BCI went out of business before the contract ended, and the UFW was unable to organize the workers, who now harvest lettuce for independent growers.

Strawberries have been a success story, with acreage expanding as consumers treat them as an everyday fruit. The UFW launched a campaign to organize strawberry workers in 1995–96 and attracted national leaders to its rallies in Salinas and nearby Watsonville; AFL-CIO President John Sweeney called the UFW's strawberry campaign the most important union organizing drive in the United States in April 1997. The UFW asked the Agricultural Labor Relations Board for permission to supervise an election at the largest U.S. strawberry grower in 1998, but lost to an ad hoc committee of workers that had formed an independent union.[11] The Agricultural Labor Relations Board ordered a round of elections in which the UFW won the right to represent workers at Coastal Berry, but the UFW has been unable to organize most strawberry workers. The UFW maintains an office in Salinas and participates in the deliberations on land use and water that will shape the future of Salinas agriculture.

VENTURA COUNTY

The coastal county of Ventura is best known to Southern Californians for its beaches, military bases, and bedroom communities intimately linked to Los Angeles. In the 1980s and 1990s, Ventura County became an economic center in its own right, with a concentration of high-tech and biotech companies in the eastern half of the county and agriculture and the military the mainstays in the western half of the county. Growth and change in the 1980s and 1990s were associated with slightly higher wages and often fewer benefits for the average 20,000 farmworkers in Ventura County, but many families fell behind because housing prices increased far more than earnings.

Ventura County had a population of 753,197 in 2000, including 252,000 Hispanics, making it the 12th largest county in California; most residents live in its southern half. The county has 10 incorporated cities—Camarillo, Fillmore, Moorpark, Ojai, Oxnard, Port Hueneme, Santa Paula, Simi Valley, Thousand Oaks, and San Buenaventura (Ventura)—and another eight towns. Hispanics make up more than 50 percent of the population in five cities and towns: El Rio, Fillmore, Oxnard, Piru, and Santa Paula.

Two-thirds of white residents in Ventura County live in cities that are at least 70 percent white, while a third of Latinos live in communities that are at least 70 percent Latino. Oxnard, Santa Paula, and Fillmore are the major ports of entry for immigrants who work in agriculture and are home to over half the county's Latinos. Oxnard, for example, added 18,000 residents in the 1990s, the net effect of losing 11,000 whites and 1,000 blacks and gaining 30,000 Hispanics.

Ventura Agriculture and Jobs

Ventura County is a major agricultural county, with its $1.4 billion in annual farm sales in 2004 dominated by strawberries, nursery stock, lemons, and avocados. Ventura ranks 10th among California farm counties. Its annual farm sales are equivalent to those of Utah.

According to the 1997 census of agriculture, Ventura County had 1,261 farms that hired a total 22,561 workers (a worker employed on two farms is counted twice). Most of Ventura County farms hired only a few workers. The 248 farms that hired 10 or more workers accounted for 88 percent of directly hired workers. About 57 percent of directly hired workers were employed less than 150 days on the responding farm, and 86 percent of directly hired seasonal workers were employed by 132 farms that hired 10 or more workers directly (the census of agriculture does not obtain employment information from labor contractors and custom harvesters).

Between 1985 and 2000, civilian employment in Ventura County increased 37 percent (table 5.3), and farm employment rose at about the same pace. However, there was a marked contrast between farm production employment (employees directly hired by farming operations) and farm services employment (employees hired and brought to

Table 5.3. Ventura County Agricultural Employment, 1985–2000

	1985	1990	1995	2000	1985–2000 change (%)
Civilian unemployment	22,600	21,100	28,500	18,700	−17
Civilian employment	287,400	349,300	353,600	392,700	37
Farm employment	14,400	16,700	17,000	19,600	36
Production	9,300	10,700	9,600	11,900	28
Services	5,100	6,000	7,400	7,700	51
Food and kindred products employment	2,200	1,700	1,600	1,300	−41

Source: California Employment Development Department. http://www.calmis.ca.gov/htmlfile/subject/indtable.htm.

farms by contractors and custom harvesters). Average farm production employment rose 28 percent, while average services employment rose 51 percent. Employment in the nonfarm processing food and kindred products industry, which involves canning and freezing fruits and vegetables, fell 41 percent.

Most farmworkers in Ventura County were born in Mexico, often in Michoacan, Guanajuato, and Jalisco. The newest farmworkers are often Mixtec-speaking indigenous peoples from Oaxaca, and many settle in the Port Hueneme area. Some Mixtecs have little education, but others were teachers and professionals in Oaxaca. Most farmworkers live in conventional housing—single-family homes, apartments, and mobile homes—but housing is expensive: the 40th percentile fair market rent for Ventura County was $1,000 a month for a two-bedroom apartment in 2002. Thus, many families double up in housing units, leading to overcrowding, especially in Oxnard and in mobile home parks around Santa Paula and Fillmore. The earnings–housing cost gap for farmworkers is among the highest in the state—an income of almost $3,400 a month is needed to keep housing that costs $1,000 a month at 30 percent of earnings.

From Unions to Contractors

Growth and change in Ventura County agriculture between 1980 and 2000 have not improved conditions for most farmworkers. Citrus was the major commodity for most of the 20th century and, in the late 1970s and early 1980s, most lemon and orange pickers in the county were unionized. When the federal minimum wage was $2.65 an hour in 1978, many pickers had piece-rate earnings of $5 to $7 an hour and worked 800 to 1,200 hours a year. In 2002, the state minimum wage was $6.75 an hour, and many farmworkers earned $7 to $10 an hour. However, hours of work fell, reducing annual earnings.[12]

Ventura County agriculture had a wide range of employer co-ops providing services to midsized lemon and orange growers. The co-op principle was extended to labor management, meaning professional managers were often hired to organize workers for the lemon harvest. The Ventura County citrus industry was a pioneer in providing housing and other services to farmworkers and, in many cases, their families.

Between 1942 and 1964, the packinghouses that controlled citrus harvesting hired bracero workers who lived in barracks-style camps. Packinghouses demonstrated progressive personnel practices by introducing a piece-rate wage system that aimed to standardize worker earnings even as grove conditions changed. Workers earned more per bin when there were fewer lemons and trees were taller, and less when yields were higher and trees shorter. Ironically, Central Valley citrus, which developed in the late 1950s, was less dependent on braceros, largely because by the time there was significant production, the U.S. Department of Labor was more strictly enforcing bracero wage and housing rules, and Central Valley packinghouses thus turned to farm labor contractors to obtain harvest workers from among local residents.

The mid-1960s were a time of transition for labor in Ventura County, as lemon growers responded to the end of the bracero program by reducing quality standards and increasing worker productivity with improved clippers, lighter synthetic bags, aluminum ladders, and larger bins. Employers introduced or increased worker benefits by offering health, pension, and UI benefits to stabilize the workforce— that is, to keep the same workers returning year after year.

The largest of the labor co-ops was the Coastal Growers Association (CGA), founded in 1961 and the subject of UC extension bulletins in 1974 and 1980 that described best-practice, win-win situations for employers and workers. CGA harvested lemons for its grower-owners and became large enough to achieve economies of scale in recruiting, housing, and deploying lemon harvesters. After the bracero program ended, CGA developed modern personnel practices to recruit, reward, and encourage the return of the best pickers. As a result, CGA pickers saw their average piece-rate earnings rise from $1.77 an hour in 1965 to $5.63 an hour in 1978, and average annual earnings rose from $267 (for 151 hours) in 1965 to $3,430 (for 609 hours) in 1978.[13] The Consumer Price Index doubled between 1965 and 1978, while hourly wages tripled and annual earnings rose almost thirteenfold. Productivity rose sharply, from 3.4 boxes an hour in 1965 to 8.4 boxes an hour in 1978.

CGA was able to add benefits for its fewer, more productive pickers and keep the costs of picking for its grower-owners low. The wage cost of picking each box of lemons rose 25 percent between 1965 and 1978,[14] while the total cost of harvesting a box rose 73 percent with the introduction of benefits that ranged from paid vacation to health insurance, still less than inflation. CGA and the other labor co-ops built or rehabilitated housing for workers,[15] and their success in developing a professional harvest workforce contributed to a declining interest in mechanization. An industry magazine, the *Citrograph*, reported in January 1978 that the number of harvest mechanization projects fell from 31 in the early 1960s to 7 in 1977.[16]

The UFW organized the workers employed at most of the labor co-ops in the spring of 1978. The background for the union drive was a bumper crop of lemons in 1976–77 that reduced grower prices and meant there was no increase in picker piece rates in 1978. In March 1978, after a dispute over the piece rate in one grove, CGA workers voted 897–42 to have the UFW represent them. The transition to collective bargaining seemed smooth, as CGA negotiated a three-year agreement that raised piece rates by 22 percent and other co-ops signed agreements, so that 70 percent of Ventura lemons were picked under UFW contracts by the end of 1978.

Unions continued to demand wage increases in the early 1980s while illegal immigration was rising. Some foremen at the co-ops became labor contractors, organized crews of recently arrived unauthorized workers, and offered to harvest fruit cheaper than the co-ops, whose aging and unionized workers had higher benefit/overhead costs. In some cases, the new contractors were able to pay union piece rates to their younger workers and make a profit because they offered no fringe benefits, which unauthorized solo men did not value as much as the workers with settled families employed by the co-ops. As in the Imperial Valley, the UFW called a strike in 1981 to support its demand for a significant wage increase, and many growers withdrew from CGA and the other labor co-ops and turned to contractors to obtain lemon pickers.

By the late 1980s, a decade after lemon harvesters were organized successfully, none were represented by unions. The historical question is whether the demise of the labor co-ops was the result of "excessive" UFW wage and benefit demands or of illegal immigration. Both played a role, but illegal immigration was probably the major factor, since without unauthorized workers contractors may have been unable to compete with the co-ops.

By 2001, growers reported that the labor supply was tightening, but there were no new efforts to organize new co-ops that would help to balance labor demand and supply to minimize the number of pickers. Unless there is a severe labor shortage, it seems unlikely that the lemon industry will reorganize the co-op system. The major farm labor trends in the county include the changing composition of the farm workforce, which includes more Mixtecs and Zapotecs, many of whom do not speak Spanish.

6

THE CHANGING FACE OUTSIDE CALIFORNIA

ATLANTIC SEABOARD

The third wave of immigrants to the United States from 1890 to 1914 brought southern and eastern Europeans to eastern and midwestern cities. Most of these newcomers did not become farmers or farmworkers, but there were crews of newcomers who traveled daily or seasonally from cities such as Philadelphia to fields nearby to be farmworkers (Hahamovitch 1997).

The fact that horses provided the power to move people and goods in eastern cities led to two farming industries that relied on horse manure: the poultry industry of the Delmarva Peninsula (the area where Delaware, Maryland, and Virginia converge), where farmers used manure as fertilizer to produce grain for chicken feed; and the mushroom industry of southeastern Pennsylvania, where farmers used horse manure for mushroom production. Workers in these industries were primarily white and black until the 1980s, when fewer and larger farms, Central Americans fleeing civil wars, and more nonfarm job options quickly changed the face of the workforce.

Delmarva Poultry Processing

The Delmarva peninsula, which includes all of Delaware, the eastern shore of Maryland, and one Virginia county, is the sixth-largest poultry processing region in the United States; the 625 million broilers raised there accounted for about 9 percent of the broilers processed in the United States in the mid-1990s.[1] Delmarva poultry employs an estimated 21,000 people, 7,000 self-employed farmers who raise chickens and 14,000 workers who process them.[2]

Most farmers have 5,000 to 25,000 chickens and raise them under contract for one of six Delmarva poultry processors. The processor provides the chicks and feed (corn and soybean meal) and controls farming practices, while farmers provide the sheds, heat, electricity, and labor to feed the chickens and remove the waste. After about 10 weeks and 10 pounds of feed (feed accounts for more than half the cost of production), chickens reach a farm weight of 5.3 pounds. Uniform birds make disassembly easier, and the trend toward uniformity has been hastened by fast food restaurants that want uniform chicken parts to cook in automated fryers.

To be processed, chickens are caught, placed in cages, trucked to a plant, hung, and then processed at a rate of 70 to 90 birds per minute. Live chickens are conveyed to machines that shock them and cut off their heads so they bleed before defeathering and foot removal. Chickens are rehung for evisceration and USDA inspection and then cut into breasts, legs, and other parts by machine. In contrast to meatpacking workers, who use knives to cut meat from carcasses moving by them, poultry workers often position chickens for machines to do the cutting.

Most of the Delmarva processing plants are relatively old, and recent renovations have placed more emphasis on dealing with waste to protect the environment rather than saving labor.[3] A midsized poultry processing plant employs about 700 workers and processes a million birds per week, with 330 workers on each of two shifts and a 60-person sanitation crew that cleans equipment overnight. Most poultry processors require newly hired workers to provide work authorization documents and to undergo drug tests; the drug tests eliminate more U.S. than immigrant workers in Delmarva.

Delmarva poultry processing plants have been relatively isolated from nearby cities such as Baltimore and Philadelphia. However, when beach resort areas expanded in the 1980s and offered alternative jobs to the African Americans who dominated poultry processing, immigrants from the San Marcos area of Guatemala area settled out of the migrant farmworker stream to fill jobs in the plants. Many Guatemalans applied for asylum and were allowed to stay in the United States after courts agreed that the U.S. government allowed foreign policy concerns to dictate which Central Americans were recognized as refugees.

Wages in the plants are about 60 percent of the average for manufacturing workers, $7 an hour in the mid-1990s or $14,000 a year. The largest Delmarva plants pay slightly higher wages and are not unionized, but the United Food and Commercial Workers union represents workers at some smaller firms. All plants have significant worker turnover, with 20 to 50 percent of employees leaving in less than one year, but employers and employee advocates disagree about why turnover is so high. Worker advocates assert that employers encourage turnover to save on benefit costs[4] and to avoid the worker solidarity that could lead to unionization, while employers say the turnover is due to workers' personal preferences, including changing jobs or employers after extended visits to their countries of origin or to work alongside recently arrived friends and relatives at other plants.

Most poultry plants are always hiring workers, and most participate in the Basic Pilot employee verification program, which involves submitting new immigrant employees' documentation to immigration authorities to determine eligibility to work in the United States. Most workers present valid documents—only 1 percent of the data submitted for verification was rejected in the late 1990s—but the documents submitted may not belong to the worker presenting them. Some unauthorized workers falsely claim to be U.S. citizens, which exempts them from the verification process. Unannounced workplace inspections in the 1990s found that up to 10 percent of the workers were unauthorized.

The center of Delmarva poultry is Georgetown, Delaware, a city of 4,400 that was one-third Hispanic in the mid-1990s. The poultry companies do not provide housing for workers, so most live in subdivided, often crowded private housing. Private vans provide rides to work, and there has been a proliferation of services, from restaurants to money transfer firms, catering to the Hispanic workforce. The city and county have added sports facilities and international travel signs to promote integration and are encouraging public employees to learn Spanish.

Pennsylvania Mushrooms

Mushrooms are the major farm commodity in nearby southeastern Pennsylvania, with half the state's mushrooms produced in Chester County in suburban Philadelphia. Mushrooms grow in two-story cinder block "houses" with about 8,000 square feet of growing space, and most have three tiers or levels of wooden trays about 8 feet wide and 50 feet long.[5] Mushrooms are generally picked three times before removing the spawn for another crop, and productivity has increased from two pounds per square foot in the mid-1960s to six pounds in the mid-1990s.

Most workers are harvesters, cutting four to eight trays an hour that each have 10 pounds of mushrooms; most houses have lights, so pickers do not wear helmets with lights. Piece-rate wages in the mid-1990s were $0.12 a pound or $1.20 per box, which enabled most pickers to earn $5 to $8 an hour and $200 to $400 a week. Many pickers live in grower-provided housing at no charge or pay lower-than-market rents to their employers. Chester County had an estimated 2,200 to 4,000 mushroom harvesters in the mid-1990s, and most were Mexicans who replaced Puerto Ricans. There is some tension between Mexicans and Puerto Ricans in Kennett Square, the self-proclaimed mushroom capital of the world; some Puerto Ricans accuse the Mexicans of displacing them, and some Mexicans are jealous of Puerto Ricans' eligibility for welfare benefits.

Carolina Tobacco and Crabs

North Carolina tobacco and crab processing represent an alternative way to get seasonal work done: using guest workers. Since the mid-1990s, half the legal guest workers admitted to fill U.S. farm jobs have been employed on tobacco farms, and North Carolina is the number-one state employing H-2A workers. Farm employers of H-2A workers do not pay Social Security and UI taxes on the wages earned by H-2A workers in the state, and the workers, contrary to program rules, often pay for their own recruitment in Mexico.

The crab processing industry in North Carolina and nearby states relies on H-2B workers from Mexico. There are fewer than 60 crab processing plants in the seaboard states, and they have only about 2,500 workers, but half are Mexican women with H-2B visas. Most crab employers provide housing for H-2B workers, charging them $15 to $25 a week for beds in mobile homes or ex-motels, and require the H-2B workers to repay the $100 cost of bus tickets from Mexico to the Carolinas.

Blue crab processing involves women wielding knives who extract crabmeat for a piece rate of $1.50 to $2 per pound.[6] Crab pickers average about $40 for eight-hour days, but the defining characteristic of the work is uncertainty: the number of crabs and thus the hours of work and earnings are highly variable. There have been efforts to mechanize the extraction of crabmeat, but mechanization is more likely to succeed with crabs raised by aquaculture farms than with species caught in the wild, since wild crabs vary too much in size for most machines to handle efficiently. The Atlantic seaboard states primarily deal with wild crab species.

African American women dominated the crab picking labor force until a combination of more nonfarm job opportunities and the diffusion of community colleges and thus education and training options pulled younger women in particular out of the crab plants. Some of the local workers complain that employers give priority to Mexican

H-2Bs when there is little crab available, further discouraging locals from sticking with the industry.

IOWA AND MIDWEST MEATPACKING

The changing face of Iowa and other midwestern states is a consequence of changes in the U.S. meat processing industry. The $70 billion slaughtering and processing industry turns cattle, hogs, sheep, and poultry into meat and other products on disassembly lines that have long been staffed by immigrants. However, falling real wages and rising immigration over the past quarter-century have changed the face of many small towns in the Midwest.

The meat processing industry has experienced several major changes in the past several decades. First has been the shift from pork and beef to chicken. Between 1970 and 2000, average per capita annual consumption of beef declined from 80 to 65 pounds, but chicken consumption almost doubled, from 28 to 53 pounds, in part because the real prices of poultry products declined by 55 percent between 1960 and 2000. The second major change has been the shift from unionized slaughterhouses in cities such as Chicago to processing plants in rural areas that raise and fatten cattle and hogs. Third has been the shift of preparation of meat products from retail stores to processing plants, where wages are lower and workers can prepare boxed beef as well as cut-up, seasoned, and sometimes cooked meat products that are more consumer friendly.

The 491,000 meat processing employees in 2000 accounted for about 7 percent of nondurable U.S. manufacturing employment. The share of meat processing employees in nonmetropolitan areas rose from less than 50 percent in 1980 to 60 percent by 2000. The Hispanic share of the meat processing workforce has also been rising, from 15 percent in 1990 to 35 percent in 2000.

A restructuring of the labor force accompanied the restructuring of the meat processing industry. Historically, the meatpacking industry offered relatively high wages to unskilled, often non-English-speaking workers because urban meatpacking plants had to pay wages sufficient to keep workers from leaving for other employers. In rural areas, there was less competition from other employers, and average meatpacking wages fell from a peak $15 an hour in 1979 to less than $10 an hour in the mid-1990s (both in 1992 dollars).[7]

Most of the new workforce entrants to high-turnover meat processing plants are Mexican immigrants who arrive directly from rural Mexico or move to the Midwest from elsewhere in the United States, such as south Texas. Unlike the Delmarva peninsula, where many of the first poultry processing workers were settled migrant farmworkers, mid-western states have fewer seasonal farm jobs, and most of the workers that filled farm jobs in the past were local teens. Pioneer migrants found meatpacking jobs as a result of recruiting efforts (many midwestern plants sent recruiters to south Texas) and by accident, as when migrants headed to Michigan or Wisconsin stopped in Iowa or Illinois. Once employed in the plants and settled in the area, they put out the word to family and friends, and network recruitment took over the task of filling vacant jobs.

Another industry change has been increased concentration in the raising and slaughter of animals. Fewer and larger operations dominate the industry, and many are vertically integrated, as when a feedlot is next to the slaughterhouse. As in poultry, many hogs are now raised under contract with meatpackers, so that the largest 1 percent of U.S. hog farms, each selling 50,000 or more hogs a year, accounted for about 40 percent of production in 2000. The major cost for meatpackers is the price of the animal—$0.60 to $0.70 a pound for cattle and $0.40 to $0.50 a pound for hogs. By contrast, disassembling these animals into meat products costs $0.05 to $0.10 a pound for beef and $0.20 to $0.25 a pound for pork. By 2000, retailers received about 60 percent of the average dollar spent on pork, farmers 18 percent, and processors 22 percent.

The slaughtering process is straightforward. Five-month-old hogs weighing 250 pounds are processed at the rate of 1,200 per hour, or 19,000 on two eight-hour shifts. Arriving hogs are stunned, hung by one leg, stuck with a knife to bleed, and then carried through machines that wash the carcasses and singe them to remove hair. Machines split the carcasses and remove internal organs, and workers make various cuts as the carcasses move by, suspended from overhead conveyor belts. Meat is packed in vacuum bags, which increase the usual three-day shelf life to three weeks, placed in large paperboard bins for transit, and chilled before being sent in refrigerated trucks to retail outlets.

On average, there is about one production worker for each 10 hogs a day slaughtered, so plant workforces are often 1,500 to 2,000. Few production jobs pay twice the entry-level wage, and the flat wage structure helps explain high turnover. Workers that want an extended vacation in their home villages may not care that they have to start over again at the bottom when they return. Some worker advocates claim that plants encourage high turnover to save on benefit costs and because some state and local governments provide subsidies for newly hired workers for their first six months of employment.

Meatpackers in countries with less access to migrant workers have pioneered the development of labor-saving technologies. For example, a government agency, Meat New Zealand, developed the world's first robotic machines for meat processing.

Employer Sanctions

Many meatpacking employees—estimates range from 25 to 35 percent—are not authorized to work in the United States. During the late
1990s the unemployment rate in states such as Nebraska dipped under
2 percent, and high-turnover meatpacking plants offered bonuses of
$200 to $300 to anyone, current employees or recruiters, who brought
workers to the plant that stayed at least 60 days. Some meatpackers
ran ads in Mexico, offering workers authorized to be employed in the
United States $8 an hour, bus fare to the United States, and medical
and dental insurance.

Regional INS officials accused meatpackers of fostering illegal migration and decided to test a new method to remove unauthorized workers
from the plants in Nebraska. Under Operation Vanguard, the INS
subpoenaed I-9 employee verification forms from 111 meatpacking
plants in Nebraska and checked the employee information against
Social Security Administration (SSA) and INS records. The INS told
meatpackers to ask employees with discrepancies to clear them up
before agents came to the plant to interview them. Agents interviewed
only employees about whom there was doubt during workplace visits.

In 51 meatpacking plants, typically small operations, there were no
discrepancies and thus no plant visits. However, the other 60 plants
had one or more employees with discrepancies between the data on
the I-9 form and the data in SSA/INS databases. These 60 plants had
24,148 employees, including about 4,100 with discrepancies. Of the
workers with discrepancies, 3,152 quit when their employers informed
them of the discrepancies; the INS interviewed 1,042 in May 1999 and
arrested 34. During the six months that Vanguard was most active,
immigration authorities spent some $528,000 to open 3,500 jobs for
legal workers, versus $234,000 spent for one 1992 raid on a Monfort
Inc. plant in Grand Island, Nebraska, that resulted in 307 arrests.

The INS emphasized that checking employee records is far cheaper
and less disruptive than workplace raids. However, migrant advocates
and anti-migrant groups both protested. The advocates complained
that irregular migrants lost jobs and had no way to support their
families and that the high turnover caused by periodic INS inspections
meant many workers did not work long enough to qualify for benefits
such as health insurance. Anti-migrant groups complained that the
program identified but did not remove irregular migrants. This criticism, plus complications involving the use of the Social Security database to enforce immigration laws, led to a suspension of the process.
The Vanguard approach resumed after the September 11, 2001, terrorist
attacks, primarily to check on workers employed in critical infrastructure facilities such as airports, seaports, and power plants.

Other attempts to enforce employer sanctions in meatpacking have also largely failed. In December 2001, the federal government charged Tyson Foods Inc., the largest poultry processor in the United States, with recruiting illegal workers for 15 of Tyson's 57 poultry processing plants in the Midwest and South. Tyson managers allegedly arranged to have workers smuggled into the United States and paid them $100 to $200 before arranging transportation from the border to its plants. The government charged that Tyson "did cultivate a corporate culture in which [management condoned] the hiring of illegal alien workers . . . to meet its production goals and cut its costs to maximize Tyson profits."[8]

The INS used undercover agents, wiretaps, and paid informants in the two-and-a-half-year investigation to send a message to the meatpacking industry. The assistant United States attorney in Chattanooga said, "It's much more productive, we think, to attack the source, the companies that recruit these illegals, than to pursue endless prosecutions of illegals at the border."[9] Tyson admitted that it used temporary employment agencies to recruit foreign workers for its plants but took no responsibility for its actions. The government alleged that "Tyson utilized workers that were hired and provided to Tyson by temporary service agencies . . . well knowing that most of these workers were unauthorized for employment within the United States."

Tyson promised to vigorously defend itself, and it did. Tyson asserted that the government offered to settle the case for $100 million, and it refused to pay because the previous highest payment for a violation of immigration laws was $1.9 million. John Tyson, president of Tyson Foods, said that his firm was only doing what other firms did to get needed workers: "America is going to keep growing. There are going to be jobs available, and people are going to need to keep coming to this country if there [are] not going to be enough people around here" to take the jobs.[10]

In April 2002, the stakes in *United States v. Tyson Foods Inc.* were raised when a suit was filed on behalf of four U.S. citizen employees under the federal Racketeer Influenced and Corrupt Organizations (RICO) law seeking triple damages for "the amount of wages that were depressed" by the presence of unauthorized workers. A RICO lawsuit must first prove that the underlying crime was committed and then show there was a racketeering enterprise, such as a pact between a smuggler and an employer.

After a seven-week trial in 2003, a jury acquitted Tyson of charges that its plant managers conspired to hire unauthorized workers to boost Tyson profits, making them, in the prosecution's phrase, "pinstriped coyotes." Tyson's defense was that a few rogue managers hired unauthorized workers despite company policy to hire only legal workers.

The company's attorney said, "It is not the fault of this company that there are approximately eight million undocumented workers in the United States. It is not our fault that the systems that the government has set up for hiring employees is not perfect. If the prosecutors and the government want a perfect system, the government ought to be designing it."[11] The jury believed Tyson. However, the 6th U.S. Circuit Court of Appeals in June 2004 ruled that former Tyson employees could pursue their RICO suit against Tyson.

Meat and Migrants

Immigration has changed the face of the midwestern towns with meat-packing plants, and the responsibility of meatpackers for the demographic changes their employment practices bring is still being debated. Storm Lake, Iowa, a city of 8,800, became 10 percent minority within a decade because of two meatpacking plants with 2,000 employees. The school system requested that local meatpackers pay for English as a Second Language classes and bilingual teachers, but the meatpackers pointed to their payrolls as their contribution to the local economy. Residents of the nearby town of Spencer cited Storm Lake's experience as a reason for the town's refusal to grant a zoning variance so a meatpacking company could open. During the January 2000 presidential primary, the Federation for American Immigration Reform ran ads highlighting the changing face of Storm Lake. The reaction to the ad campaign was mixed. Some Storm Lake residents said that Storm Lake benefited from immigration and diversity, while others said they preferred a stable or shrinking population to diversity and the higher taxes associated with caring for needy immigrants.

Garden City underwent similar demographic changes after ConAgra Beef Processors and IBP (formerly Iowa Beef Processors) opened or expanded meatpacking plants in southwestern Kansas that employed 3,500 workers. The sudden influx of Southeast Asians and, later, Mexicans into a city of 25,000 put pressure on available housing. Many newcomers found housing in mobile home parks, which sometimes brought complaints from local residents. When a Christmas Day 2000 fire closed the ConAgra plant for six months, the local unemployment rate tripled until the plant reopened.

The city of Rogers in northwestern Arkansas is sometimes cited as a model for accommodating immigrants who work in poultry processing plants. Between 1980 and 2000, the population of Rogers almost doubled to 40,000, and Hispanics became 15 percent of residents. Rogers adopted an ambitious plan to integrate Hispanics "in all neighborhoods, locations and areas," and a Rogers bank developed a plan that enabled many two-earner families earning $7 an hour at area poultry plants to qualify for mortgage loans. Mayor John Sampier was credited with organizing sports leagues that enabled the newcomers to get to know established residents, but in 1998 voters elected to replace him with Steve Womack—who demanded "zero tolerance" toward unauthorized foreigners and insisted that legal newcomers "speak the language" and conform to community norms.[12]

There are mixed reactions to the changing face of midwestern towns. On the one hand, migrants have preserved local industries and stabilized populations, ensuring that churches and schools do not shrink further. On the other hand, residents complain that the migrant influx has been associated with more crime, higher social assistance costs, and the difficulties of integrating newcomers from very different cultures. Those who oppose meatpackers say they do not want to preserve rural towns if the cost is turning them into rural ghettos. Those who favor migrants say that the diversity they bring will revitalize rural areas.

PART 3

21ST CENTURY CHALLENGES

If current trends continue, the farmworkers of tomorrow are growing up today outside the United States. The major migration management challenge is to determine how to match these foreign farmworkers with U.S. farm jobs.

The extremes of the policy debate—closed and open borders—are a convenient starting point to consider the alternatives. Those opposed to slowing or stopping the flow of newcomers fear sharply higher wages that could disrupt rural economies. With land and other asset prices based on the assumption that migration will continue and hold labor costs stable, tighter borders could force some farmers and farm-related industries out of business, accelerating stagnation in rural areas that are struggling to hold people and jobs.

On the other hand, if migrants continue to arrive in rural America with their families but earn only poverty-level wages that discourage their U.S.-educated children from following their parents into fields and factories, rural America may find itself on an immigration tread-mill. Under this scenario, migrants would continue to arrive and fill jobs that U.S. workers shun, and rural America could once again become a reservoir of workers for whom economic mobility requires geographic mobility, meaning that to get ahead workers and their children would have to move to cities, as large numbers did between 1920 and 1970.

Previous chapters have reviewed the seemingly endless debate over agriculture's need for migrants, emphasizing that there are alternatives to high levels of illegal immigration and that most Americans would not notice even sharp increases in farm wages because they do not spend much on fresh fruits and vegetables, and farm wages are a small share of the retail price of produce. Chapter 7 turns to three major proposals to fix the farm labor problem: President Bush's earned guest worker program, a bipartisan earned immigrant program, and an agriculture-specific program that would allow unauthorized farmworkers to become probationary and eventually regular immigrants. Chapter 8 addresses fundamental questions about the U.S. migrant labor force.

7

THE QUEST FOR AGJOBS

Obtaining seasonal farmworkers has long been a challenge. Farmers worry about the cost and availability of seasonal workers, while workers employed only seasonally fear they will not earn enough during the time that they work to support themselves until the next season. Few researchers, regulators, or journalists who deal with farm labor would consider the current U.S. system one that other countries should emulate. What, then, is being proposed to deal with the farm labor problem, and what are the likely consequences of the major proposals?

IRCA: SAW-RAW AND H-2A

The starting point for most immigration and integration proposals affecting rural America is the fact that over half of U.S. farmworkers, and a significant share (at least a quarter) of workers in farm-related industries (such as meat and poultry processing), are unauthorized. In September 2003, farm employer and worker advocates announced a compromise proposal, the Agricultural Job Opportunity, Benefits, and Security Act of 2003 (AgJOBS), to legalize the status of farmworkers and to offer them and their families a path to immigrant status (Martin 2005).

AgJOBS is a compromise. It lays out a path to legal immigrant status for unauthorized farmworkers, thus satisfying worker advocates, while making it easier for farm employers to obtain guest workers. If AgJOBS were enacted, the farm labor market would be tugged in opposite directions. Most of those employed in the fields should be legally authorized to work in the United States, but legal status may also make farmworkers and their children more mobile in the U.S. labor market. If the newly legalized leave farmwork and are quickly replaced by legal guest workers, the farm workforce may be more legal than it has been for decades, but it may also be more "foreign," in the sense that future guest workers may come from Mexico as well as other countries and workers would be expected to leave the United States when their seasonal jobs end.

The AgJOBS proposal is rooted in a never-implemented part of the 1986 Immigration Reform and Control Act (Martin 1994). IRCA created two legalization programs. The one based on residence gave immigrant status to 1.7 million unauthorized foreigners who had been in the United States since January 1, 1982, and the one based on employment gave legal status to 1.1 million unauthorized foreigners who did at least 90 days of farmwork in 1985–86.

Farmers feared that newly legalized workers would quickly find nonfarm jobs, leading to farm labor shortages, and won two concessions in IRCA. First, the H-2 program was made more employer friendly; it was converted into the H-2A program, but it still required farmers to have their need for legal guest workers certified and to provide free housing to out-of-area farmworkers. This was not sufficient insurance for California farmers, who feared unions and did not have housing. So they won a second avenue to obtain legal foreign workers, the Replenishment Agricultural Worker (RAW) program, which allowed a number of legal foreign workers to "float" in the U.S. farm labor market. Farmers could hire these workers without proving to the U.S. Department of Labor that U.S. workers were unavailable and would not have to provide housing to them. The RAW workers could earn immigrant status if they did at least 90 days of farmwork a year for three years.

Fears of farm labor shortages prompted three major federal agencies, the Departments of Agriculture, Justice, and Labor, to develop systems for estimating the supply of and demand for farmworkers and to move quickly to admit H-2A and RAW workers to avoid crop losses due to lack of labor. The H-2A program expanded as expected, but only from 20,000 to 25,000 a year between the mid- and late 1980s. The program then began to decline as Florida sugarcane growers mechanized their harvest in response to a class-action suit over the wage system for cane cutters. After reaching a low in the mid-1990s, the number of certified H-2A farm jobs rose sharply, reflecting the use of such temporary agricultural workers to harvest tobacco (table 7.1).

The Departments of Agriculture and Labor established surveys to determine if there were labor shortages due to the rapid exit of newly

Table 7.1. U.S. Department of Labor H-2A Certifications, 1985–2000

		Certified Jobs in the Major Commodities		
	Certified farm jobs[a]	Sugar cane	Tobacco	Sheep
1985	20,682	10,017	831	1,433
1986	21,161	10,052	594	1,043
1987	24,532	10,616	1,333	1,639
1988	23,745	10,751	2,795	1,655
1989	26,607	10,610	3,752	1,581
1990	25,412	9,550	4,666	1,677
1991	25,702	7,978	2,257	1,557
1992	18,939	4,271	3,080	1,522
1993	17,000	2,319	3,570	1,111
1994	15,811	1,419	3,720	1,305
1995	15,117		4,116	1,350
1996	19,103		9,756	1,366
1997	23,562		14,483	1,667
1998	34,898		16,984	1,961
1999	41,827		16,206	1,443
2000	44,017		14,554	1,865

Sources: U.S. Department of Labor (1985–2000).
[a]Farm jobs the Department of Labor requires be filled with H-2/H-2A workers.

legalized SAWs but found none. The question before the Commission on Agricultural Workers (CAW), established to evaluate IRCA's farm labor provisions, was whether the RAW program should be allowed to expire as scheduled in 1993, under the theory that the agricultural labor market should have adjusted to IRCA by then. Some farmers' representatives argued that RAW should be maintained to provide labor insurance, but the majority of commissioners pointed to signs of a glut of farmworkers—falling real wages, few reports of successful union organizing and bargaining, and reports of two and three workers applying for each farm job—to argue successfully that the RAW program should expire unused (CAW 1993).[1]

The RAW program expired, but farmers did not give up the quest for a less burdensome guest worker program. Almost before the ink was dry on the Commission on Agricultural Workers' conclusions—that that there was "a general oversupply of farm labor nationwide" and that, "with fraudulent documents easily available" (1993, xx), employer sanctions were not deterring the entry or employment of unauthorized workers—farmers had bills introduced in Congress to establish an alternative to the H-2A program. In 1994 and 1995, bills were introduced to allow farmers to attest that they needed foreign workers and give the U.S. Department of Labor seven days to accept or reject their attestations, not enough time to try to recruit U.S. workers, especially in other states.[2]

The U.S. Commission on Immigration Reform tried to head off this push for a new guest worker program, concluding that "a large-scale agricultural guest worker program . . . is not in the national interest . . . . Such a program would be a grievous mistake."[3] President Clinton echoed this sentiment with a June 23, 1995, statement: "I oppose efforts in this Congress to institute a new guest worker or *'bracero'* program that seeks to bring thousands of foreign workers into the United States to provide temporary farm labor."[4]

These statements did not prevent bills from being introduced to make the H-2A program more employer friendly. For example, Senator Larry Craig (R-ID) introduced the Agricultural Work Force and Stability Protection Act in January 1997 to eliminate the need for farm employers to recruit U.S. workers before being certified to employ H-2A guest workers, arguing that the declining number of jobs certified by the Department of Labor in the mid-1990s reflected a bureaucratic and anti–guest worker mindset. INS workplace enforcement in the Washington apple industry in 1996–97 prompted Representative Richard Doc Hastings (R-WA) in April 1997 to suggest that the INS grant "consideration" to farmers during harvest season by not enforcing laws against illegal immigration vigorously: "there has to be some consideration and recognition if somebody is working. . . . If somebody is not working, that's where our [INS enforcement] emphasis ought to be."[5]

In May 1998, the INS launched operation Southern Denial during the Vidalia onion harvest, apprehending 21 of the estimated 3,500 to 5,000 peak harvest workers in a one-day operation on two farms.[6] In the year before the operation, the INS met with growers, and they promised to hire legal U.S. workers or to recruit H-2A guest workers. However, a grower-sponsored organization, Vidalia Harvesting, withdrew an application for H-2A workers in spring 1998, citing the cost of complying with H-2A program rules and potential suits by worker advocates, and did not follow through on a plan to pay the farm labor contractors who normally bring crews of workers from Texas a recruiting fee of $8 per worker (General Accounting Office 1998, 3).

Onion farmers' congressional representatives protested, with Senator Paul Coverdell (R-GA) asserting that "extreme enforcement tactics against Vidalia area onion growers . . . [are interfering with] honest farmers who are simply trying to get their products from the field to the marketplace."[7] The INS stopped enforcement in exchange for employer pledges to hire only legal workers and to make available to the INS their employment records. The General Accounting Office (GAO) concluded that the growers knew many of their workers were illegal, but disagreed with DOL on the prevailing wage: growers said it was $0.70 to $0.75 per 60-pound bag of onions picked, while DOL insisted it was $0.80 per 50-pound bag of onions picked, or 30 percent higher (GAO 1998, 10). GAO noted that, if growers participated in the H-2A program, they would no longer be able to charge U.S. and H-2A workers for housing and would have to provide workers' compensation insurance for their workers.

THE AGJOBS COMPROMISE

Pressure from growers for an alternative to the H-2A program led the Senate to approve the first version of AgJOBS as an amendment to the Commerce–Justice–State Department appropriations bill in July 1998 on a 68–31 vote.[8] This version of AgJOBS included a long-time goal of farmers, to keep DOL from supervising their recruiting efforts by establishing worker registries in each U.S. farming area. These registries, located at local Employment Service offices, would register only legally authorized workers. Farm employers would submit job offers to their local registry. If an employer requested 100 workers and the Employment Service had only 40 workers in the registry to respond, then the employer would be permitted to recruit 60 foreign farmworkers. In part because of a threatened presidential veto, the conference committee removed AgJOBS from the appropriations bill.[9]

Senate approval of AgJOBS by a 2–1 margin was a wake-up call for worker advocates. For the first time, the Mexican government had weighed in on behalf of a grower-supported bill. Mexican Labor Secretary Jose Antonio Gonzalez said in March 1999 that Mexico has "been thinking about analyzing what occurred between the United States and Mexico years ago, when there was a regulated interchange of workers," and pointed to the Mexico–Canada seasonal worker program as a model. The U.S. Department of Labor, citing President Clinton's 1995 statement,[10] made strong statements opposing a new guest worker program.[11] However, to head off more proposals for a new guest worker program, DOL streamlined the H-2A program by shortening the time before their need date that farmers had to notify DOL, thus reducing recruiting times.

AgJOBS was reintroduced in 2000 with a new twist: a path to immigrant status for unauthorized workers who continued to do farmwork. Worker advocates had demonstrated that they could block proposals that simply made it easier for farmers to recruit and employ legal guest workers, so growers included what advocates wanted—allowing newly legalized farmworkers to be free agents in the U.S. labor market and offering them a path to immigrant status. However, to ensure that newly legalized farmworkers would not suddenly abandon farmwork, they would have to do farmwork for several years to earn immigrant status.

The elections of Vicente Fox in Mexico and George W. Bush in the United States in 2000 changed the guest worker debate. Fox toured Canada and the United States after his election and proposed European Union–style freedom of movement, which put immigration and guest worker issues on the front page. The House Immigration and Claims Subcommittee in September 2000 approved a grower-friendly bill on a 16–11 vote that would have created a new guest worker program, prompting worker advocates to begin serious negotiations with grower representatives on a compromise proposal. In December 2000, they agreed on an earned legalization program, under which unauthorized workers would receive temporary legal status that could be converted to immigrant status if they continued to do farmwork over the next six years.[12] Worker advocates were pleased that unauthorized workers and their families could become legal immigrants, while employers received the changes they wanted in proposed revisions to the H-2A program and thought the continuing work requirement would prevent the immediate departure of experienced farmworkers. However, Senator Phil Gramm (R-TX) termed the compromise an amnesty and blocked approval of AgJOBS in the waning days of the Clinton administration.[13]

Presidents Bush and Fox met in February 2001 and established a binational "migration working group" to create "an orderly framework for migration that ensures humane treatment [and] legal security, and dignifies labor conditions." Mexican Foreign Minister Jorge Castaneda said, "The final goal is to regularize the situation of those Mexicans who are without documents."[14] He went on to say that Mexico's four-pronged immigration agenda included legalization, a guest worker program, ending border violence, and exempting Mexico from visa quotas. In perhaps an unfortunate summary of Mexican demands, Castaneda said, "It's the whole enchilada or nothing."[15]

During the spring and summer of 2001, Mexican and U.S. officials met to discuss how to improve conditions for unauthorized Mexicans in the United States, the top foreign policy goal of the Fox administration. Several proposals were introduced to legalize farm and other workers, and the debate centered largely on whether the United States should grant currently unauthorized workers a guest worker status, an immigrant status, or a temporary resident status that could eventually be turned into an immigrant status, as proposed in AgJOBS.[16]

Presidents Bush and Fox met in Washington, D.C., on September 5, 2001, and Bush tried to dampen hopes for quick progress on a new immigration program by saying, "Immigration reform is a very complex subject. This is going to take a while to bring all the different interests to the table. . . . Our desire is to make it easier for an employer looking for somebody who wants to work and somebody who wants to work to come together, but that in itself is a complex process."[17] Fox had hopes for a quick agreement, saying, "The time has come to give migrants and their communities their proper place in the history of our bilateral relations. . . . We must, and we can, reach an agreement on migration before the end of this very year [2001 . . . so that] there are no Mexicans who have not entered this country legally in the United States, and that those Mexicans who come into the country do so with proper documents."[18]

The September 11, 2001, terrorist attacks stopped the debate over new guest worker proposals, but in September 2003, Senators Edward Kennedy (D-MA) and Larry Craig (R-ID) introduced a revised AgJOBS proposal that eventually attracted 64 Senate and 115 House cosponsors. Under this version of AgJOBS, unauthorized foreigners who did at least 575 hours or 100 days of farmwork (one hour or more constitutes a day of work) in any consecutive 12-month period between March 1, 2002, and August 31, 2003, could receive a six-year Temporary Resident Status (TRS) that would grant them the right to live and work in the United States.[19] TRS workers could earn regular immigration status by performing at least 2,060 hours or 360 days of farmwork in a six-year period ending in 2009, including at least 1,380 hours or 240 work days during their first three years and, in at least three of the six years, at least 75 days of farmwork a year. The spouses and minor children of TRS workers would not be deportable if they were in the United States, but they would not be allowed to work legally until the TRS worker became an immigrant (i.e., a legal permanent resident).[20]

This version of AgJOBS also satisfied grower demands by making the H-2A program more employer friendly. For example, instead of having the DOL certify the need for foreign workers, farmers would simply attest that they needed foreign workers, and DOL would have to approve employer attestations if they were filed at least 28 days before the farmer-determined date workers were needed. The burden of proving labor shortages would be shifted to DOL, which would have to authorize the admission of H-2As if local workers were not available at least 14 days before the farmer's need date.

Most farm employers do not offer housing to the seasonal workers they employ. Under the Kennedy–Craig version of AgJOBS, employers could provide workers with "a monetary housing allowance" if the state's governor certified that "sufficient housing" exists in the areas where guest workers were to be employed. Workers would receive a housing allowance from employers equivalent to the "statewide average fair market rental for existing housing for metropolitan or nonmetropolitan counties." With four workers sharing a two-bedroom unit in California's major farm counties, where average rents range from $600 to $1,000 per month, the housing allowances would be $150 to $250 per worker, per month.[21]

Worker advocates and grower representatives pushed for congressional approval of AgJOBS during 2004, aiming to have a strong bipartisan approval in the Senate to overcome stronger opposition from so-called anti-immigrant Republicans in the House. However, during the summer of 2004, the Senate did not vote on AgJOBS despite 63 cosponsors, reportedly because the White House asked Republican Senate leaders not to allow a vote to avoid antagonizing anti-migrant Republican voters before the November 2004 elections. The Senate vote on AgJOBS finally came on April 19, 2005; the vote was 53–45 to attach it to an emergency military spending bill (60 "yes" votes were needed). Senator Larry Craig (R-ID) promised to attach AgJOBS to another must-pass bill.

WHAT NEXT FOR AgJOBS?

If AgJOBS is enacted, farm labor discussions will be dominated by the possible application of over a million unauthorized workers for temporary legal status, the registration of their dependents, and the systems established to monitor their farmwork. Farmers will likely test how easy it is to obtain legal guest workers via the further streamlined H-2A program, and some of the farm labor debate may shift from federal to state levels as governors come under pressure to certify sufficient housing for farmworkers is available, while worker advocates call attention to state applications for federal housing funds to demonstrate shortages.

Even if more than a million foreigners apply for the new TRS, there are still likely to be unauthorized farmworkers. Under the SAW program of 1987–88, the best estimates were that 400,000 farmworkers would be eligible, and the government printed 800,000 application forms. About 1.3 million foreigners applied, and the government approved 90 percent of them because it had no way to disprove that the applicant did the requisite farmwork. Under AgJOBS, the burden of proof is reversed and placed on the applicant, and many of the unauthorized may not be able to satisfy the requirement that they did at least 100 days of farmwork.

No one knows how many unauthorized farmworkers there are and how many might apply and qualify for TRS. Table 7.2 provides three estimates of the number of unauthorized in 2005: 1.2 million, 1.4 million, and 1 million.

However, many of these unauthorized workers would not qualify for legal status because they have not done either 575 hours or 100

Table 7.2. Unauthorized Farmworker Estimates, 2005

Percent unauthorized workers in crops/livestock	58/20	66/33	50/10
Hired workers	2,500,000	2,500,000	2,500,000
Crop workers	1,800,000	1,800,000	1,800,000
Unauthorized workers	1,044,000	1,200,600	900,000
Livestock workers	700,000	700,000	700,000
Unauthorized workers	140,000	233,100	70,000
Total unauthorized workers	1,184,000	1,433,700	970,000

Source: Authors' calculations.

days of farmwork. The NAWS found that U.S. crop workers averaged 120 to 155 days of farmwork a year in the 1990s, but found that unauthorized workers had fewer average days—indeed, only half of unauthorized workers did 90 or more days of farmwork in the DOL survey, in part because many had arrived within the previous two years (Carroll et al. 2005). Thus, just as IRCA's SAW program did not legalize all unauthorized farmworkers in 1987–88, AgJOBS is unlikely to legalize all unauthorized farmworkers today.

OTHER LEGALIZATION PROPOSALS

President Bush unveiled a Fair and Secure Immigration Reform (FSIR) proposal in January 2004 that would permit unauthorized but employed foreigners to become guest workers who are free to travel in and out of the United States while their work visas are valid—a maximum of six years. When the work visas expire, guest workers would return to their countries of origin, unless a U.S. employer sponsored them for an immigrant visa. Since U.S. employers may currently sponsor unauthorized foreigners for immigrant visas, current procedures for adjusting to immigrant status would not change.

Bush has long been a proponent of a new guest worker program, saying several times that he wants a program to "match willing foreign workers with willing U.S. employers when no American can be found to fill those jobs."[22] However, the availability of American workers has long been debated, which is why the certification process involving supervised employer recruitment of U.S. workers was established. The Bush plan would deem the fact that an employer hired unauthorized migrants proof that no American worker is available.

In his February 2005 State of the Union speech, Bush said, "It is time for an immigration policy that permits temporary guest workers to fill jobs Americans will not take, that rejects amnesty, that tells us who is entering and leaving our country, and that closes the border to drug dealers and terrorists," but did not offer any legislative proposal to turn these ideas into law.[23] White House aides have said their guest worker program, which regularizes currently unauthorized workers for six years, could function as follows. U.S. employers would acknowledge an unauthorized worker's employment history in a letter or affidavit. The worker would take this letter to Department of Homeland Security, pay a fee of $1,000 to $2,000 and undergo a security check, and receive a renewable three-year work permit. During this maximum six years, the registered guest worker could enter and leave the United States, but family members would have no special privileges to visit the United States.

The Bush proposal offers no clear path to immigrant status, with administration officials emphasizing that "there is no linkage between participation in this program and a green card. . . . One must go home upon conclusion of the program" and then apply for an immigrant visa, perhaps with the support of the U.S. employer.[24] Bush has suggested increasing the number of permanent immigrant visas available for foreigners sponsored by U.S. employers to fill vacant jobs, currently 140,000 a year for the foreign workers and their families, with a limit of 10,000 for unskilled workers. Thus, if Bush adds 100,000 employment-based immigrant visas a year, a tenfold increase, it could take 10 years to convert 1 million former unauthorized foreign workers into immigrants.

The Bush plan deals with unauthorized workers currently in the United States and workers outside the United States who would like to enter to fill U.S. jobs. To determine if there are sufficient U.S. workers, Bush has suggested that U.S. employers advertise job vacancies for at least two weeks on a new Internet labor exchange and justify refusing to hire any U.S. workers who respond to the ads. After following this procedure, the U.S. employer could go to any foreign country and recruit guest workers, who would receive three-year renewable work visas such as those issued to unauthorized workers in the United States. To encourage foreigners to stay at home until they are recruited, guest workers outside the United States would not have to pay the $1,000 to $2,000 charged to unauthorized workers in the United States. All guest workers would have a new incentive to return home: credits in their home country's pension system for their contributions to U.S. Social Security.

Most U.S. employers welcomed the Bush plan because it legalized their current unauthorized workers and offered an easier way to obtain future guest workers. However, critics pointed to the failure of President Bush to follow his concepts with a bill and said the proposal aimed more to win points with U.S. Hispanics than to spur Congress to act. Some migrant advocates said that unauthorized foreigners would be unlikely to pay to register if they receive only a three-year renewable work permit, but a poll of 4,800 Mexicans in the United States—conducted at Mexican consulates over six months as Mexicans, mostly unauthorized, applied for identity documents—found that 79 percent would sign up for "Bush work visas" that required them to leave the United States eventually. However, 51 percent of the unauthorized who were questioned said they wanted to stay in the United States permanently (Suro 2005).

Most Democrats agree that legal is better than illegal, but they want the end status for currently unauthorized foreigners to be legal permanent residency, not guest worker status. During the late 1990s, as farmers were introducing bills to make it easier to obtain guest workers, congressional Democrats were introducing bills to have another residence-based legalization program, as under IRCA. For example, after the AFL-CIO in 2000 called for an end to enforcing employer sanctions laws and a general legalization program for unauthorized foreigners in the United States, Representative Luis V. Gutierrez (D-IL) introduced the U.S. Employee, Family Unity and Legalization Act, which would have granted temporary legal status to persons in the United States before February 6, 2000, and immediate immigrant status to persons in the United States before February 6, 1996. The legalization date would then have rolled forward a year in each of the next five years, eventually encompassing all those in the United States illegally when the bill was introduced.

There was little support in Congress for another legalization bill based on residence, leading Democratic presidential candidate John Kerry in 2004 to endorse a more mainstream proposal that required unauthorized foreigners to earn an immigrant status. One major proposal introduced in 2004 with strong Democratic backing was SOLVE, the Safe, Orderly, Legal Visas and Enforcement Act, which would allow unauthorized workers who had been in the United States at least five years, worked at least two years, and could pass English, background, and medical checks to apply for immigrant visas. Those in the United States less than five years could apply for a five-year "transitional status" and, after satisfying the work, English, and other requirements, could apply for "earned immigrant status."[25] To deal with backlogs of relatives waiting to join family members in the United States, SOLVE would have exempted close relatives from numerical limits on family-based immigration and granted immediate admission to applicants for immigration visas who had been waiting more than five years, regardless of per country limits.

In general, Democrats favor immigrants over guest workers, and under SOLVE, the number of low-skilled guest workers would have been capped at 350,000 a year, with the U.S. Department of Labor certifying employers' needs for guest workers. To protect guest workers, the enforcement of labor laws would increase significantly, and guest workers could apply for immigrant visas after two years of U.S. employment. Most migrant advocates and unions supported SOLVE over the Bush guest worker proposal, citing the clear path to immigrant status, faster family unification, and limits on guest workers.

In May 2005, Senators John McCain (R-AZ) and Edward Kennedy (D-MA) introduced a bipartisan plan for immigration reform, the Secure America and Orderly Immigration Act of 2005. McCain–Kennedy would, among other things, create a new "Essential Worker Visa Program," making 400,000 new H-5A and H-5B visas available to essential workers inside and outside the United States, with the cap adjusted in response to labor market conditions.

Like the Bush proposal, the McCain–Kennedy bill deals with foreign workers inside and outside the United States. Unauthorized foreigners in the United States on May 12, 2005, can apply for H-5B visas if they have a U.S. work history and pass background checks. However, to qualify for an immigrant visa, they must continue working in the United States, pass additional security and background checks, and pay a substantial fee or fine of at least $2,000. Foreigners outside the United States with a U.S. job offer can pay $500 for an H-5A visa valid for three years and renewable once. At the end of six years, the workers will either return home or get in line for an immigrant visa. The H-5A and H-5B visas are portable, meaning that the guest worker can change U.S. employers and enter and leave the United States, but he or she cannot remain jobless in the United States for more than 60 days.

Employers may sponsor H-5A and H-5B workers for immigrant visas after they have been employed at least four years in the United States, and workers may apply on their own for immigrant visas after five years of U.S. employment. The number of immigration visas available for economic/employment reasons will increase from 140,000 to 290,000 a year (including family members). However, to free up more immigration visas for family unification, immediate relatives of U.S. citizens will no longer be counted against the 480,000 annual cap on family-sponsored immigration visas, and the income requirement for sponsoring family members will be reduced from 125 percent of the federal poverty level to 100 percent.

The McCain–Kennedy bill proposes enforcement changes to discourage the employment of unauthorized workers. For example, a new electronic work authorization system would replace the current paper-based I-9 system, and the Department of Labor would gain new authority to conduct random audits of employers to ensure they comply with labor laws. The McCain–Kennedy proposal aims to promote circular

migration by requiring Mexico and other countries to enter into migration agreements with the United States that will help control the flow
of their citizens to jobs in the United States and encourage the reintegra-
tion of their citizens returning home.

AgJOBS and Immigration Reform in Context

U.S. immigration policy has been based on the premise that foreigners
should enter and work in the United States legally. Employer sanctions
in the mid-1980s and the border control buildup after the mid-1990s
aimed to accomplish this control goal. However, in the absence of
internal enforcement, the result has been something of a Darwinian
border-crossing test: those who elude the Border Patrol find it relatively
easy to obtain false documents and U.S. jobs, and the U.S. employers
that hire them face little risk of fines.

The starting point for most immigration reform proposals is a broad
perception that the current immigration system is broken. Most proponents of change are dissatisfied that 3 percent of residents, 50 percent
of farmworkers, and 10 percent of low-wage workers are not authorized
to be in the United States. However, disagreement on how to fix the
immigration system, whether reform should be comprehensive or
piecemeal, and how to avoid having reform increase illegal flows has
stymied political change.

President Bush, in arguing that legal is better than illegal, favors a
temporary worker program for unauthorized workers inside and outside the United States, at least implicitly acknowledging that the border
should but cannot be controlled and that unauthorized workers have
a place in the U.S. economy. Turning such general propositions into
concrete plans requires hard choices about issues that range from what
employers must do before hiring guest workers to how the government
will monitor them inside the United States. One proposal, embraced by
McCain–Kennedy, is to issue work visas that do not tie guest workers to
a particular employer, under the theory that this protects the worker
by allowing him or her to leave bad employers.

The Bush, SOLVE, and McCain–Kennedy proposals aim to deal com-
prehensively with immigration reform, tackling all industries and all
countries of origin. AgJOBS represents a piecemeal approach, since it
deals only with agriculture and farmworkers. Despite winning the
support of farmer and worker advocates and the majority of senators—
and being touted as a test of earned legalization and other concepts
included in the more comprehensive reform proposals—the Senate did
not approve AgJOBS, primarily because House Republicans denounced
it as an amnesty. Even if AgJOBS were enacted, it would deal with

only 1 million of the 7 to 8 million unauthorized foreign workers in the United States. It would also leave agriculture with the unauthorized workers who do not qualify.

Immigration reform is hard, but delaying reform is likely to make the eventual resolution of the problem more difficult. Since IRCA's legalization in 1987–88, there have been three major changes in Mexico–United States migration patterns that will complicate reform efforts. First, the origins, destinations, and composition of Mexican migrants have become more diffuse. Migrants come from more states in Mexico, including more rural and urban areas, and more Mexican migrants are women. Once in the United States, Mexicans move to more U.S. states, where they work in an ever-wider range of nonfarm industries and services. Once established in the United States, unauthorized Mexicans are more likely to stay because they realize there is no future in rural Mexico and because the difficulty they face reentering the United States illegally encourages settlement rather than back-and-forth migration.

The second change is a significant new influx of indigenous Mexicans, such as Zapotecs and Mixtecs, who speak languages other than Spanish, including Mixteco, Zapoteco, Trique, and Nahuatl. These indigenous migrants from southern Mexico are sometimes called the new-new migrants. Much poorer than average Mexicans, new-new migrants tend to start at the bottom of the U.S. job ladder, in the most seasonal farm jobs. Their lack of Spanish leads personnel systems that have adapted to Spanish-speaking workers to adjust further, and adults and children speaking Indian dialects raise new issues for health care facilities, police, and schools in migration areas.

The new-new indigenous migrants are further down the skill ladder than most Mexican migrants, but the number of highly skilled Mexicans in the United States is rising, a third change in migration patterns. About 10 percent of all people born in Mexico have moved to the United States, as have 15 percent of all Mexican-born workers. However, about 17 percent of all Mexicans with high school degrees, and an even higher percentage of those with college degrees, are believed to have emigrated. The rising number of better-educated Mexican migrants, as well as the fact that many Mexicans move directly to nonfarm jobs and industries, may change the popular connection between Mexican migrants and agriculture. If Mexicans eventually bypass the agriculture port of entry, U.S. farmers may turn to Asia for seasonal workers, allowing history to repeat itself; the first major group of seasonal farmworkers in the West was the Chinese.

8

IMPORTING WORKERS, INTEGRATING IMMIGRANTS

This concluding chapter tackles several fundamental questions, beginning with a long-debated issue: Is agriculture a unique industry that has a legitimate long-term need for exceptions from general labor and immigration laws? Thomas Jefferson and other Founding Fathers praised family farms on which farmers and their families did the work, but they also tolerated slavery so plantations had the seasonal workers to produce cotton and tobacco for export to Europe. Family farms became fewer and larger with mechanization, and slavery and share-cropping ended, but for most of the 20th century the U.S. government approved or tolerated Mexico–United States migration outside normal immigration laws to provide western agriculture a seasonal workforce.

As Americans consider whether importing Mexican farmworkers is simply another chapter in the largely successful immigration story or whether it is more likely to lead to a new rural poverty, it is important to remember three facts. First, most U.S. agriculture conforms to the family farm ideal of the farmer and his family working the land they own. The system of large farms dependent on crews of seasonal workers applies primarily to fresh fruits and vegetables. Their sales are about a sixth of U.S. farm sales, suggesting that five-sixths of U.S. agriculture would not be affected by ending immigration exceptions for agriculture. Second, when access to guest workers has been curbed in the past, agriculture adjusted, and, in the case of processing tomatoes, these adjustments increased production and lowered costs to consumers. Third, we do not know whether the immigration to rural America will result in rural ghettos or a rural renaissance. There is more poverty, but the integration process has not been under way long enough to allow a definitive assessment of what will happen to migrants and their children. Some policymakers are convinced policy can make a difference, and this book highlights actions that governments can take to avoid the transfer of rural poverty from Mexico to the United States.

ARE GUEST WORKERS NEEDED?

Should agricultural exceptionalism in immigration policy continue in the 21st century, and if so, what form should it take? This debate is not a new one. In 1909, President Theodore Roosevelt's Country Life Commission reported that "there is a growing tendency to rely on foreigners for the farm labor supply, although the sentiment is very strong in some regions against immigration" (President's Commission on Migratory Labor 1951, 19). The Country Life Commission went on to emphasize that "the best farmers usually complain the least about" labor shortages and recommended "that farming itself must be so modified and organized as to meet the labor problem halfway" (22).

Farm labor has long been recognized as a problem. Farmers argue that they provide jobs in a unique and vital industry for workers who otherwise would not be employed. Reformers counter that agriculture is and should be treated as other industries, and that its employees should expect to earn above-poverty-level incomes. The farmers' argument for being exempt from general labor and immigration laws rests on the seasonality inherent in crop production. Ideal seasonal workers, they suggest, are persons who do not want or cannot get "normal jobs," and foreigners without other U.S. job options fit this description perfectly.

Seasonality and the subsequent need for guest workers was expected to diminish as the labor supply tightened once the bracero program ended in 1964 and rising wages spurred mechanization. In the virtuous circle sketched in the 1960s, there would be few newcomers from abroad, and farming would change like other industries that offer seasonal outdoor jobs, such as logging, shipping, and construction. This virtuous circle appeared in the 1970s, when farm wages rose and fringe benefits spread, mechanization eliminated heavy lifting jobs, and farmers expanded the production of fruits and vegetables despite rising labor costs. Leading farm labor economists concluded that "the concept of a career in hired farmwork is becoming increasingly recognized" (Fuller and Mamer 1978).

This virtuous circle soon gave way to a vicious circle of labor contractors hiring newly arrived unauthorized migrants. Farm labor markets unraveled in the early 1980s for many reasons, but immigration reform in 1986 offered a second chance for farm labor reform to turn farm jobs into careers. Unions, migrant advocates including the Catholic Church, and growers established competing organizations to help unauthorized farmworkers legalize their status. However, less than 10 percent of the 1.3 million SAW applicants used one of these organizations to legalize, far less than were helped by farm labor contractors who provided letters asserting that the applicant worked for them.

Immigration exceptions such as the bracero and SAW programs have made agriculture a major industry for unskilled Mexicans, making the seasonal farm labor market a major port of entry for migrants. Growers argue that this system of newcomers arriving and doing several years of seasonal farmwork before they find better jobs must continue because, without them, fresh fruits and vegetables would become luxury items. This argument may have held more sway in the past, when working families spent 30 to 40 percent of their earnings on food, almost all of which was consumed at home. But today, the cost of food eaten at home accounts for less than 8 percent of the average household's annual expenditures, and most food spending is not for fresh fruits and vegetables picked by migrant workers.

Household spending data make it clear that cheap farmworkers are not the reason Americans have cheap food. According to the Bureau of Labor Statistics' Consumer Expenditure Survey, there were 112 million "consumer units," with an average of 2.5 persons, 1.4 earners, and two vehicles in 2002.[1] Average consumer unit income before taxes was $49,400 ($46,900 after taxes), and expenditures averaged $40,675.

These consumer unit or household expenditures included $5,375 for food (13 percent), with spending split between the $3,100 spent on food eaten at home (8 percent of total expenditures, or $60 a week) and $2,300 spent on food eaten away from home. To put this food spending in perspective, other significant expenditures were housing and utilities, $13,300; transportation, $7,800; health care, $2,350; apparel, $1,700; entertainment, $2,100; cash contributions, $1,300; and tobacco products, $320.

Most analyses focus on food consumed at home, since spending for food consumed away from home includes the atmosphere and service at the restaurant. The largest food-at-home expenditures were for meat and poultry, $800 a year, and nonalcoholic beverages such as soft drinks, $255, with milk and cream another $130. Expenditures on fresh fruits ($178 a year) and fresh vegetables ($175) totaled $353, or $6.80

a week.[2] In one sign of spending priorities, the average household spent more on alcoholic beverages ($376) than on fresh fruits and vegetables ($353).

Americans spent a total $40 billion on fresh fruits and vegetables in 2002. Even though strawberries are picked and placed directly into the plastic containers in which they are sold, and iceberg lettuce gets its film wrapper in the field, farmers receive an average of only 16 percent of the retail price of fresh fruits and 19 percent of the retail price of fresh vegetables. This means that the $353 paid by the average household for fresh fruits and vegetables generated $61.73 in revenue to farmers.[3] Farmers, of course, do not pay all their revenue to farmworkers. Farm labor costs are typically less than a third of farmer revenue, so consumers who pay $1 for a pound of apples, or $1 for a head of lettuce, are giving 16 to 19 cents to the farmer and 5 to 6 cents to the farmworker.

The farmworker wages and benefits embodied in fresh fruits and vegetables cost the typical household about $20 a year. What would happen if the influx of immigrant workers slowed, farm wages rose, and consumers paid for the increase in farm labor costs? One guide is the 40 percent wage increase won by the UFW for grape pickers after the bracero program ended. The average hourly earnings of field and livestock workers were $8.45 in 2002, according to a USDA survey of farm employers (USDA 2002); a 40 percent increase would raise them to $11.83.

Suppose this farm wage increase were passed fully to consumers. In that case, the 5- to 6-cent farm labor cost of a pound of apples or a head of lettuce would rise to 7 to 9 cents, and the retail price would rise by 2 to 3 cents. For a typical U.S. household, a 40 percent increase in farm labor costs translates into a 2 to 3 percent increase in retail prices and raises total spending on fruits and vegetables by $8 a year, from $353 to $361. However, for a typical seasonal worker employed 1,000 hours a year, earnings could rise from $8,450 to $11,830 a year, or from below the federal poverty level for an individual to above the poverty level.

Since consumer spending and production cost data do not support the argument that fresh fruits and vegetables would be luxuries without migrants, why is the argument so familiar? The answer lies in the farmland market. According to the census of agriculture, there were 5 million acres of trees and vines and 4 million acres of vegetables. Land prices vary significantly, but using a very conservative estimate of $7,500 an acre, these 9 million acres are worth $67 billion.

What would happen to the value of fruit and vegetable land if there were a 40 percent increase in farmworker wages? The value could fall by a third, to $5,000 an acre or $45 billion. This potential $20 billion decline in asset values explains why requests for contributions to grower political action committees are often prefaced with remarks such as "We know how tough it is to earn a decent return growing apples or oranges, but investing in Washington to get the workers we need is the best investment we can make." If fewer farmworkers raised farm labor costs, consumers would hardly notice the difference, but land owners would.

INTEGRATING MIGRANTS

If the United States continues to import workers without options to fill seasonal farm jobs, what will happen to them and their children? One strategy for alleviating poverty among farmworkers and their children is to invest in public programs that promote social and economic mobility, and by extension, health and well-being. Federal policymakers have paid comparatively little attention to immigrant integration and much less to integration in the nation's rural areas. However, the thrust of recent antipoverty policies that promote marriage and work makes an uncertain fit for immigrants, many of whom are already married and work. The absence of an integration policy is notable not just because of high flows, but also because the poverty, hardship, and low education levels of farmworkers have spread to agricultural areas throughout the United States.

Introducing integration programs that effectively reach migrant workers and their families presents special challenges. Migrants are dispersed, and many live in regions where tax bases can be low and social safety nets are thin. But a core set of social programs begun during the 1960s remains in place, including Migrant Education, Migrant Head Start, Migrant Health, and Job Training (Martin and Martin 1993). Reformers created these programs to help U.S. farmworkers and their children escape from farmwork in an era when farm jobs were expected to disappear because of mechanization. Although mechanization was limited, most U.S. farmworkers and their children got out of seasonal farmwork, and the programs have largely been retained over time. However, the $1 billion a year in federal funds may be insufficient for the new immigrants who now are the core of the seasonal farm workforce.

The most significant development in federal integration policy may be in education, where the 2002 No Child Left Behind Act requires schools to identify, serve, and be held accountable for the performance of limited English proficient (LEP) and immigrant children. Schools with significant shares of LEP students, such as those in many agricultural regions, disproportionately fail to meet required federal academic progress standards.

Today, one in nine U.S. residents is an immigrant. One in five children is the child of an immigrant, and more than one in four low-income children is the child of an immigrant. Most of these children are U.S. citizens: 75 percent of children with noncitizen parents are themselves citizens who live in mixed-status families; two-thirds of the children of the undocumented are citizens. Mixed-status families pose peculiar integration challenges, since parents and children can have different membership claims, and unauthorized parents may be reluctant to seek benefits such as health insurance and food stamps for which the children may be eligible. Seasonal farmworkers pose even more challenges, since many have mixed-birth families, with one or more children born in the United States and others born abroad. Other families are mixed-residence families, in which children remain abroad.

Immigrants dispersed beyond the six traditional gateway states (California, Florida, Illinois, New Jersey, New York, and Texas) in the 1990s, and this heavily agriculture-led labor migration creates its own integration challenges. Many of the new destinations have little experience settling newcomers and not much infrastructure. Many new destination states are known for their low taxes and low benefits, which result in thin safety nets for migrants who are often young, less-educated, and less likely to speak English well than the immigrant population in traditional receiving states.

Marriage and work are major antidotes for poverty, but they may not be for newcomer migrants, because many of them are already married and working. Children of immigrants living in two-parent families were twice as likely to be poor (44 versus 22 percent) as the children of natives in 2002, and two-thirds of farmworker children who live with both parents remain poor. Farmworkers tend to be poor despite working: immigrants are one in nine U.S. residents, one in seven U.S. workers, and one in five low-wage workers, earning less than two times the minimum wage. The Urban Institute's National Survey of America's Families found that 41 percent of working immigrant families, compared with 21 percent of their native counterparts, had low incomes in 2002, reflecting limited language skills and low levels of education.[4] Immigrants are 11 percent of U.S. residents but 40 percent of U.S. workers with less than a high school degree and 75 percent of U.S. workers with less than a 9th grade education (Capps, Passel, and Fix 2003). The educational qualification of farmworkers is even lower. These low education levels translate into higher levels of economic hardship among children of immigrants than the children of natives.

In 1996, welfare reform legislation limited legal noncitizen eligibility for federal means-tested benefits, including Medicaid, the State Children's Health Insurance Program, Temporary Assistance for Needy

Families, Supplemental Security Income, and food stamps. Estimates based on the Current Population Survey found that benefit use rates differ widely by program (Fix and Passel 2002). For example, legal noncitizen rates of TANF use were lower than citizens' in 1994 and fell further through 2002. This low use of TANF is important because it is a gateway to other work supports, such as child care subsidies, that over time have become largely restricted to TANF recipients. There was a 55 percent drop in TANF use rate by naturalized citizens and a sharp rise in the number of naturalized citizen families with incomes under 200 percent of the poverty level, suggesting that naturalization is not translating into more access to means-tested benefits. Citizen use of food stamps fell sharply between 1994 and 2002, and noncitizen use fell faster and further. The one exception to the steep decline in the use of safety net programs is Medicaid. There are rising rates of Medicaid use among legal noncitizens between 1994 and 2002, reflecting enactment of the State Child Health Insurance Act as well as outreach to immigrant and other minority communities. Nonetheless, low-income children of immigrants remain far more likely to lack health insurance than low-income children of natives.

High levels of poverty and disadvantage among the children of immigrants are evident among K–12 students. In 1970, the poverty rates among first- and second-generation children of immigrants were roughly comparable to those of non-Hispanic whites; by 2002, they had climbed to the high levels of African American youth. Rising poverty among the children of immigrants has been paralleled by high levels of school-based segregation. More than half of LEP students attend schools where 30 percent or more of their fellow students are also LEP, and schools with large enrollments of LEP students frequently fail to meet new standards for annual progress under the No Child Left Behind Act. The act requires schools to report limited English proficient student scores on standardized tests, imposes tough sanctions on schools if LEP students do not make progress, and requires that bilingual and English as a second language classrooms have qualified teachers. Will the inability of schools to meet No Child Left Behind requirements lead to student success or to higher drop- and push-outs, so that the scores of lagging students do not count?

Finally, a quarter of the children of immigrants have at least one undocumented parent, producing both integration and labor market issues that comprehensive immigration reform proposals must tackle. Most of the immigration reform proposals are silent on integration, and none includes anything like the $4 billion in federal assistance to state and local governments under IRCA, the State Legalization Impact Assistance Grant program.

NEW SOLUTIONS OR NEW PROBLEMS?

The United States has experience dealing with the rural poverty that led to a great migration off the land from the 1940s to the 1960s. But it has less experience with the current rural poverty arising from rural Mexicans moving to rural America. Past rural poverty was characterized by out-migration from farming areas suffering from overproduction and low prices, not from areas with rising farm fruit and vegetable production and with farmers complaining of labor shortages despite double-digit unemployment rates. Low wages and frequent unemployment characterize the new rural poverty, making seasonal farm jobs attractive primarily to those who face worse conditions at home.

The immigrant farmworkers who arrive to fill seasonal jobs on U.S. farms do not stay in agriculture, and their children educated in the United States avoid following their parents into the fields. If immigrant farmworkers and their children wind up in small towns and cities in areas that have not experienced immigration for a century and are ill-equipped for the task of turning poor newcomers with little education into Americans, will their integration be a success? The integration challenge is even greater because of current federal policies. For example, the beefed-up Border Patrol has raised the cost of being smuggled into the United States, but not enough to stop migrants from trying to enter. Once in the United States, migrants stay longer because of the cost and difficulty of reentry. Their children, typically born in the United States and enrolled in U.S. schools, often know what they do not want: the U.S. jobs their parents have. But these children may not receive the education or opportunities for the jobs they do want in the rural towns where they live.

There are technological alternatives to seasonal workers, but farmers unsure about freer trade in an era of stiffer global competition with lower-wage countries often prefer to have government continue to make immigration and labor exceptions rather than invest in an expensive mechanization alternative. Is there a way to couple immigration exceptions for agriculture with policies that promote mechanization? One option would be to introduce employer-paid fees in any new guest worker program. A farmer's decision to hire migrants rather than mechanize is an economic decision. However, one farmer alone can rarely mechanize farm tasks, since packing and processing facilities must be organized to accept hand- or machine-picked produce, but not both. If farmers paid a user fee for legal guest workers,[5] and these fees were used to promote labor-saving changes, there could be a reduction and perhaps an eventual end to the employment of guest workers. User fees are not new in agriculture, as exemplified by the fees farmers pay to promote their commodities.

Evidence shows that there is little truth to the argument that poor farmworkers are necessary to have cheap food. The annual cost savings to the typical household from having low-wage workers in the fields are less than the cost of a movie ticket. However, the eventual costs of integrating immigrants and their children who begin their U.S. journeys in American fields will, at least initially, be greater. Without comprehensive immigration reform, Americans risk the creation of a new and persistent rural poverty that will prove hard to extirpate.

APPENDIX

The econometric model used in chapter 3 to test for year-2000 employment, immigration, and poverty interactions in rural California towns consists of a block triangular system of three equations, two of which (farm employment and immigration) constitute a simultaneous sub-block that is recursively related to the third (poverty). This model corresponds to a structural partial-equilibrium theoretical model that includes immigrant labor supply, farm labor demand, and poverty outcomes. The specific form of the equation system is

$$(1) \quad FARM_t^i = \alpha_0 + \alpha_1 FOR_t^i + \alpha_2 WPOP_t^i + \alpha_3 FARM_{t-1}^i + \epsilon_{1t}^i$$

$$(2) \quad FOR_t^i = \beta_0 + \beta_1 FARM_t^i + \beta_2 POP_t^i + \beta_3 WPOP_t^i + \beta_4 FOR_{t-1}^i + \epsilon_{2t}^i$$

$$(3) \quad POV_t^i = \gamma_0 + \gamma_1 FARM_t^i + \gamma_2 FOR_t^i + \gamma_3 POP_t^i + \gamma_4 WPOP_t^i + \gamma_5 POV_{t-1}^i + \gamma_6 KIDS_{t-1}^i + \gamma_7 OLD_{t-1}^i + \epsilon_{3t}^i$$

The variables are defined in table A.1. The key dependent variables are the share of people in farm jobs ($FARM_t^i$), the share of foreign-born population (FOR_t^i), and the share of residents in households with below-poverty income (POV_t^i) in town i at time t. The central hypotheses of this paper are that (a) farm employment is positively associated with rural poverty in 2000 ($\gamma_1 > 0$); (b) farm employment stimulates migration ($\beta_1 > 0$); and (c) migration, in turn, stimulates the creation of new farm jobs ($\alpha_1 > 0$).

The stochastic error terms ϵ_k^i, $k = 1,\ldots,3$, are assumed to be distributed as approximately normal with zero mean and a variance of σ_k^2, uncorrelated across observations. Equations (1) and (2) constitute a simultaneous-equation sub-block, which was estimated using three-stage least squares (3SLS). If the errors in this sub-block, ϵ_{1t}^i and ϵ_{2t}^i, are not correlated with ϵ_{3t}^i (that is, the disturbance matrix, Σ, is block diagonal), ordinary least squares (OLS) yields parameter estimates for (3) that are optimal and identical to those obtained using full information maximum likelihood. Equation (3) was estimated using OLS.[1]

Due to lagged right-hand-side variables ($FARM_{i-1}^i$, FOR_{i-1}^i, and POV_{i-1}^i), the model requires data from both the 2000 and 1990 census years, drawing contemporaneous explanatory variables from 2000 and predetermined lagged variables from 1990. Each equation in the simultaneous system is identified, with at least as many excluded exogenous or predetermined variables as included endogenous variables. Because of this, there is no need for instruments from outside the system.

Table A.1. Definitions of Variables in Econometric Model

Variable	Definition
POV_i^i	Share of people in poverty in community
FOR_i^i	Share of foreign-born population in community
$FARM_i^i$	Share of workforce in farm jobs
POP_i^i	Total population
$WPOP_i^i$	Working-age population
$KIDS_i^i$	Share of population younger than 15 years old
OLD_i^i	Share of population older than 65 years old

NOTES

Chapter 1. Immigrants and 21st Century Agriculture

1. The history of these newcomers without other U.S. job options is told in Fuller (1939/1940) and Daniel (1981).

2. The 1965 Immigration Act substituted family ties and employer preferences for national origins in determining who gets priority to immigrate. It changed the origins of U.S. immigrants from Europe to Latin America and Asia. The massive buildup of the Border Patrol under the Illegal Immigration Reform and Immigrant Responsibility Act of 1996 made it more difficult and expensive to enter the United States illegally but did not stop unauthorized entries. As a result, the undocumented population in the United States grew faster than ever because those who succeeded in eluding the Border Patrol stayed in the United States longer than previous illegal entrants.

3. See the reports in the "Rural America" section of *Rural Migration News,* available at http://migration.ucdavis.edu/rmn/index.php.

Chapter 2. Migrants in U.S. Agriculture

1. Japan agreed not to issue passports to its citizens seeking to emigrate to the United States, and the U.S. government promised to end discrimination against Japanese in the United States.

2. Many of those from what is now India and Pakistan were Sikhs from the Punjab region, but all South Asia immigrants in the early 1900s were called "Hindoo" or "Hindu" regardless of religious affiliation.

3. Some of the Southern and Eastern European immigrants who arrived in eastern U.S. cities worked in agriculture. A report of the Dillingham Commission reported that New York farmers were "unanimous in the opinion that if it were not for the Italians it would be impossible to secure the labor necessary to carry on farming in its present scale . . . [and] when employed in gangs

under the immediate supervision of an American they are considered better than native farm labor for picking fruit, gathering beans, and for general work on truck farms." Dillingham Commission, *Immigrants in Industries*, Part 24, Vol. 2 (1910), 506.

4. The U.S. government established a handful of camps that offered better housing and services; the federal Weedpatch migrant camp in Arvin (today the Sunset Migrant Center) provided the backdrop for *The Grapes of Wrath*. After its publication, farmers accused Steinbeck of having Communist sympathies, Steinbeck received death threats, and the FBI investigated him.

5. Average hourly farmworker earnings in California, as measured by a USDA survey of farm employers, rose 41 percent, from $0.85 in 1950 to $1.20 in 1960, while average hourly factory worker earnings rose 63 percent, from $1.60 in 1950 to $2.60 in 1960.

6. Processing tomatoes are worth about 2.5 cents a pound. When tomatoes were picked in 50-pound lugs and each lug was worth $1.25, the loss was relatively minor if a lug was rejected for having too many green tomatoes or too many rocks and dirt. But with machine-picked tomatoes arriving in 25-ton truck loads, each load is worth $1,250; state-run random sampling stations are crucial to overcome the perennial struggle between growers and packers over deductions for poor quality.

7. Chavez kept the boycott in the news with a succession of high-profile visitors to Delano, California. For example, in March 1966, the U.S. Senate Subcommittee on Migratory Labor held a hearing in Delano, and Senator Robert Kennedy (D-NY) had a televised argument with the Kern County sheriff over the constitutional rights of Americans. The sheriff said he arrested UFW supporters because he knew they were about to break the law. Kennedy countered that Chavez and the farmworkers had the right to boycott and picket and not be arrested until after they had broken a law.

8. For analyses of the farm labor market, see Commission on Agricultural Workers (1993), Fisher (1953), and Martin (2003).

Chapter 3. Farm Employment, Immigration, and Poverty

1. Migration can stimulate employment through factor markets, by increasing the available workforce, altering the skill mix, and influencing technology choices, as well as product markets, by increasing the demand for consumer goods in an area.

2. Each town had fewer than 20,000 residents in 2000 and more than 8 percent of workers employed in agriculture.

3. For example, the 1990 farm employment share is an explanatory variable in the 2000 farm employment equation.

4. Mexico's average per capita income in 2000 was $5,749, but in terms of the goods this money can buy—that is, in purchasing power parity terms—this income is the equivalent of $9,100 in the United States (see World Bank *World Development Indicators*, 2000, and historical data from the CIA Factbook available at http://workmall.com/wfb2001/mexico/mexico_economy.html). Average incomes in rural Mexico, from which most California farmworkers originate, are lower than the Mexican national average.

The Mexican government does not regularly gather data on the per capita income of rural Mexico. Because of subsistence production and other issues, per capita income in rural Mexico is difficult to measure. The Mexico National

Rural Household Survey (*Encuesta Nacional a Hogares Rurales de Mexico—ENH-RUM*), conducted by El Colegio de Mexico and the University of California, Davis, estimates that the per capita income in rural Mexico was $1,577 in 2002. In purchasing power parity terms, it would be higher than $2,500 (authors' analysis of ENHRUM data).

Chapter 4. California: Inland Agricultural Valleys

1. Sugar levels are measured in brix (percent of sugar); most grapes are harvested at 20 to 24 brix.

2. Raisin grapes are planted in rows that run east to west, and the raisin trays are laid on the south side of the rows to maximize exposure to the sun. Temperatures on the ground between the rows reach 120°F to 140°F.

3. With the dried-on-the-vine process, the fruiting canes with this year's crop grow on the south side, on a wire about 18 inches from the main trellis, so that they can be cut by machine. The renewal canes with next year's crop grow on the north side of the row and are retrained during pruning to grow on the south side for the next harvest.

4. In such an overhead dried-on-the-vine system, space for drying grapes does not have to be saved between the rows. This one reason yields are higher.

5. Mexican gross national income per capita is adjusted to reflect purchasing power parity because, for example, housing is cheaper in Mexico than in the United States. However, Mexican-origin Parlier residents are from rural areas of Mexico, where incomes are lower (see note 4, chapter 3).

6. According to the 2000 Census, a third of families and individuals, and 41 percent of related children, had incomes below the poverty level; 15 percent reported public assistance income in 1999, and 11 percent reported Supplemental Security Income.

7. Residents in 2004 paid $9.50 a day for two-bedroom units and $10 a day for three-bedroom units, including utilities.

8. The dropout rate is from Parlier High School, which had 840 students in 2002–03: 270 in 9th grade, 250 in the 10th grade, 170 in 11th grade, and 150 in 12th grade. Some students who do not complete high school in Parlier move elsewhere.

9. "Central Valley: Jobs, Housing, Air," *Rural Migration News* 11, no. 1 (2005). http://migration.ucdavis.edu/rmn/more_entireissue.php?idate = 2005_01& number=1.

10. Diana Marcum, "An Annual Cash Crop," *Fresno (CA) Bee*, November 2, 2003.

11. In some of the farmworker cities that attracted prisons, less than a quarter of the prison employees are local residents; prison guards must have high school diplomas and pass drug tests.

12. Orange Cove closed its police department in 1986 and began to pay Fresno County $180,000 a year to have a deputy patrol the city 11 hours a day. However, saying that part-time policing prevented many businesses from opening, Orange Cove received a $3.1 million grant from the U.S. Department of Justice in 2000 to provide 24-hour police protection.

13. Orange Cove pledged to extend sewer and water services to the La Tapatia site with a $1.9 million federal grant.

14. In June 2002, 130,000 children and 91,000 adults were receiving benefits under one or more of these programs. See "California: Welfare, Housing,

Napa." *Rural Migration News* 10, no. 4 (2004). http://migration.ucdavis.edu/rmn/more.php?id = 908_0_2_0.

15. Fresno County's population is 40 percent white, 44 percent Hispanic, and 10 percent Southeast Asian.

16. George Hostetter, "Broke . . . and Broken," *Fresno (CA) Bee*, September 7, 2003. County budget data are at http://www.sco.ca.gov/ard/local/locrep/counties/0102/0102counties.pdf, p. 52.

17. Evelyn Nieves, "A Fertile Farm Region Pays Its Jobless to Quit California," *New York Times*, June 18, 2001; George Hostetter, "Welfare Recipients Get Help Getting Out of Town," *Fresno (CA) Bee*, September 7, 2003.

18. Most of the data in this section comes from the summary report of the Changing Face conference focused on Yuba City, California, September 2–4, 1999, available at http://migration.ucdavis.edu/cf/more.php?id=106_0_2_0.

19. In neighboring Sutter County, an average 6 percent of residents received cash assistance in 1998. Caseload data are from http://www.dss.cahwnet.gov/research/CalWORKsDa_388.htm, and population estimates are from http://www.dof.ca.gov/HTML/DEMOGRAP/repndat.asp.

20. One proponent of the culture of poverty is Lawrence E. Harrison, who emphasizes that many whites in Appalachia are descended from Scotch-Irish immigrants who had a culture that did not value education, a point made by David Hackett Fisher in the 1989 book *Albion's Seed*. Harrison's 1996 book *The Pan-American Dream* makes the same point about Latin Americans; in many Latin American countries, the high school dropout rate exceeds 50 percent.

21. The U.C. Cooperative Extension in 1998 estimated the cost of producing cling peaches in the Sacramento Valley at $3,800 an acre, including $600 an acre for thinning to produce fewer and larger peaches and $900 an acre to handpick and haul cling peaches. With a yield of 22 tons an acre and at a price of $210 a ton, revenues are $4,620 an acre and profits $820 an acre. Yields in the Sutter–Yuba area were 16 to 17 tons an acre in the mid-1990s (Hasey et al. 1998).

22. The $7.50 a day charge covered perhaps 50 percent of the total cost of providing this housing. Advocates also noted that migrants might avoid state-funded housing centers because of the availability of even cheaper housing with more flexible rules on the number and types of residents allowed to live there and because migrants may want to save on housing to maximize their savings.

23. Marc Lifsher, "Yuba-Sutter Region Fights Local Ills, Outside Image," *Wall Street Journal*, January 12, 2000.

24. The survey is cited in the summary report of the conference focused on Yuba City, California, September 2–4, 1999. See note 18.

25. Lifsher, "Yuba-Sutter Region."

26. Mexicali has grown rapidly, from 25,000 residents in 1955 to 438,000 in 1990 and 1.6 million in 2000, according to Mexican authorities (http://www.inegi.gob.mx/est/default.asp?c=703&e=02).

27. As early as 1915, 300,000 acres of crops were grown in the Imperial Valley, irrigated by Colorado River water. Harry Chandler's Colorado River Land Company imported Chinese workers to dig canals to irrigate the Mexican side of the Imperial Valley, but a flood in 1905 diverted the entire lower Colorado River into the Imperial Valley, creating the Salton Sea. Chandler's man-made canal is today called the New River; it begins in Mexico and flows about 60 miles north through Imperial County to the Salton Sea (Martin 2001).

28. Much of the alfalfa and grass hay is shipped to dairies in Southern California and the San Joaquin Valley or exported.

29. More information on Imperial Valley employment patterns is available at http://migration.ucdavis.edu/cf/archives1.php?id=A2001012, the web site for the conference focused on Imperial Valley, California, January 16–18, 2001.

30. The California Employment Development Department ranks employers (reporting units) by their number of employees for the third quarter of the year. In 1999, Imperial County had 4,100 reporting units; 2 had 1,000 or more employees, 6 had 500 to 999, and 14 had 250 to 499 employees. The eight largest Imperial County employers had 8,335 employees. Data available at http://www.labormarketinfo.edd.ca.gov/cgi/databrowsing/?PageID=67&SubID=138.

31. Within agriculture, employment fluctuates more from month to month for farm services employers than for farm producers. Peak–trough ratios for farm services firms are typically larger than for farm production employers; January farm services employment is 1.5 to 2.5 times August farm services employment, while January farm production employment is 1.3 to 1.8 times August farm production employment.

32. Unemployment rates are calculated for three Imperial County cities—Brawley, Calexico, and El Centro. Calexico's unemployment rate was 42 percent in September 2000. See http://www.labormarketinfo.edd.ca.gov/cgi/dataanalysis/AreaSelection.asp?tableName=Labforce.

33. Most of the data in the next three paragraphs comes from http://migration.ucdavis.edu/cf/archives1.php?id=A2001012, the web site for the conference focused on Imperial Valley.

34. In some cases, worker advocates traced labor shortage complaints to employer decisions on how to pay wages. For example, several employers complained they could not find workers to harvest asparagus. Advocates said these employers switched from piece rate to hourly wages. Workers could earn the same hourly wage harvesting lettuce or broccoli, which they preferred because asparagus requires workers to walk carefully and bend constantly.

Chapter 5. California: Coastal Agricultural Valleys

1. Most of the data in this chapter is taken from http://migration.ucdavis.edu/cf/archives1.php?id=A2000102, the web site for the Changing Face conference focused on Napa Valley, California, October 5–7, 2000.

2. A mechanical harvester, which uses a crew of five to harvest around the clock, can harvest 10 to 20 acres a day. Wine grape harvesters straddle the row and use shaking rods to dislodge the grapes, which fall onto a conveyor belt and are taken to an adjoining gondola for transport to the winery. Leaves and debris are blown away from the grapes by a fan and removed by hand.

3. The farm sales associated with each year-round-equivalent job in 1998 were $56,000 in Napa County and $50,000 in Fresno County. In other words, annual farm sales divided by average farm employment is higher in Fresno than Napa County.

4. Two vineyard-winery operations are among the 10 largest employers in Napa County. Beringer Wine Estates and Robert Mondavi Corporation each have about 1,500 acres of grapes and several hundred farmworker employees. Most of the county's top 10 employers are government agencies or health care operations. California Employment Development Department, ''Labor Market

Information: Major Employers by County," http://www.calmis.cahwnet.gov/file/MajorER/napaER.htm.

5. Napa County does not have a center that provides housing for migrant farmworker families. The state's Office of Migrant Services (OMS) provides funds to operate 26 centers with 2,100 units of housing for 12,500 migrant farmworkers and their families in 16 agricultural counties. Tenants in OMS centers must have earned most of their earned income from farmwork or food processing and have usual homes at least 50 miles from the center. In addition to on-site day care and other services, laundry facilities are provided.

6. In 2004, the charge for a bed and three meals dropped to $10 a day after the camps did not fill with workers. The St. Helena Catholic Church had allowed migrants to camp on the porch of the church for $5 a day but stopped the practice when the Napa Valley Housing Authority camps did not fill up.

7. Measure L says housing may be provided for 6 or fewer farmworkers where residential development is allowed and for 12 or fewer on agriculturally zoned land. The workers living in Measure L housing do not have to work on the property where they live.

8. Many Napa Valley workers are from Atacheo, a village of 1,500 two hours from Morelia, Michoacan. The Napa migrants raised $150,000 to build greenhouses, a turkey farm, and a stereo speaker factory in Atacheo, but these investments have so far failed to provide local jobs. Edwin Garcia, "Mexican Priest's Once-Promising Plan in Trouble," *San Jose Mercury News*, February 25, 2005.

9. Two-thirds, or 4,450, of the 6,704 births in Monterey County in 1999 were to Latina mothers.

10. Labor contractors are categorized as either farm labor and management services or personnel supply services.

11. "UFW Loses at Coastal," *Rural Migration News* 5, no. 3 (1999). http://migration.ucdavis.edu/rmn/more_entireissue.php?idate=1999_07&number=3.

12. The strong nonfarm labor market of 1998–2000 offered farmworkers with transferable skills, such as equipment operation, nonfarm job options. This mobility improved wages and put upward pressure on the hours and earnings of remaining farmworkers.

13. The number of pickers employed at CGA (based on W-2 statements issued) fell from 8,517 in 1965 to 1,292 in 1978.

14. Lemons are picked into over-the-shoulder bags and dumped into bins that hold about 1,000 pounds, but wage costs are often figured in bags or boxes: 18 bags or boxes = 1 bin.

15. Limoneira, Rancho Sespe, SP Growers, and S&F Growers, in contrast to CGA and the other co-ops that hired primarily solo male green card commuters, expanded the housing available to farmworker families.

16. *Citrograph*, January 1978, 51.

Chapter 6. The Changing Face Outside California

1. The poultry processing industry (North American Industry Classification System code 311615) comprised 311 firms with 536 establishments, according to the 2002 Economic Census. The 216,500 production workers were paid $4.2 billion, an average $19,500 each in 2002. Delaware had six plants with 4,650 production workers in 2002, and they earned an average $17,000. See the

2002 Economic Census report on poultry processing, http://www.census.gov/prod/ec02/ec0231i311615.pdf.

2. According to the 2002 Economic Census, the 189 U.S. poultry processing establishments that each had 500 to 2,500 workers had 173,000 production workers, 80 percent of the total 216,000 (non-production workers include supervisors and office staff).

3. If new plants were to be built, they would likely include far more labor-saving equipment but would also be built in the Southeast and Midwest, closer to low-cost supplies of corn and soybeans.

4. In most plants, workers do not become eligible for benefits until they have been employed 60 to 120 days.

5. In the mid-1990s, the cost of building a mushroom house capable of producing 250,000 pounds a year was about $150,000.

6. Seafood processors sell crabmeat for $6 to $13 a pound, making the labor cost of extracting crabmeat one-sixth to one-third of the wholesale price.

7. In 1982, when unions represented about half the workers in meat and poultry processing, the entry-level base wage under United Food and Commercial Workers contracts was $10.69 (MacDonald and Ollinger 2000, 24; Ollinger, MacDonald, and Madison 2000). Many meat processors demanded that the UFCW agree to a $8.25 wage, which is what many non-union plants paid, and there were 158 strikes involving 40,000 workers between 1983 and 1986. By 1987, unions represented 20 percent of meat processing workers, and there were fewer differences in wages between large and small plants and between regions.

8. Quoted in "Tyson, Sanctions," *Rural Migration News* 10, no. 2 (2004). http://migration.ucdavis.edu/rmn/more.php?id=844_0_4_0.

9. Quoted in "Tyson: Sanctions, Safety," *Rural Migration News* 8, no. 2 (2002). http://migration.ucdavis.edu/rmn/more.php?id=583_0_4_0.

10. Ibid.

11. Quoted in "Sanctions: Tyson Acquitted," *Rural Migration News* 9, no. 2 (2003). http://migration.ucdavis.edu/rmn/more.php?id=12_0_4_0.

12. Quoted in "Meat and Migrants," *Rural Migration News* 11, no. 4 (2005). http://migration.ucdavis.edu/rmn/more.php?id=1038_0_2_0.

Chapter 7. The Quest for AgJOBS

1. Admitting RAWs may not have added to the farm labor supply because over 90 percent of the almost 700,000 foreigners who registered for the program gave U.S. addresses, leading to speculation that they were already in the United States and perhaps working illegally.

2. The proposal was modeled on the H-1B program, with the farm employer's application asserting that the employer faced a shortage of labor and was paying the prevailing wage.

3. "CIR Recommends Less Immigration," *Rural Migration News* 1, no. 3 (1995). http://migration.ucdavis.edu/rmn/more_entireissue.php?idate=1995_07&number=3.

4. "Guest Workers," White House press release, June 23, 1995. Clinton's statement continued, "If our crackdown on illegal immigration contributes to labor shortages . . . I will direct the departments of Labor and Agriculture to work cooperatively to improve and enhance existing programs to meet the labor requirements of our vital agricultural industry consistent with our obligations to American workers."

5. Quoted in "INS Enforcement," *Rural Migration News* 3, no. 3 (1997). http://migration.ucdavis.edu/rmn/more_entireissue.php?idate=1997_07&number=3.

6. According to GAO (1998, 9), the INS had permission to question workers at one farm and arrested 14. At the second farm, the owner met the INS with a reporter and congressional staffer and refused permission to question workers in the field; the INS apprehended several workers who fled.

7. Quoted in "Border, Sanctions," *Rural Migration News* 11, no. 1 (2005). http://migration.ucdavis.edu/rmn/more_entireissue.php?idate=2005_01&number=1.

8. *Agricultural Job Opportunity, Benefits, and Security Act of 1998*, amendment 3258 to *Departments of Commerce, Justice, and State, the Judiciary, and Related Agencies Appropriations Act*, 1999, S 2260, 105th Cong., 2nd sess. (July 2, 1998).

9. "Congress: Guest Workers," *Rural Migration News* 4, no. 4 (1998). http://migration.ucdavis.edu/rmn/more_entireissue.php?idate=1998_10&number=4.

10. Clinton said, "When these programs were tried in the past, many temporary guest workers stayed permanently and illegally in this country. Hundreds of thousands of immigrants now residing in the U.S. first came as temporary workers, and their presence became a magnet for other illegal immigration." Quoted in "Mexico Wants Guest Workers," *Rural Migration News* 5, no. 2 (1999). http://migration.ucdavis.edu/rmn/more_entireissue.php?idate=1999_04&number=2.

11. John Fraser, the Department of Labor's Wage and Hour acting chief, testified in October 1998 that the Clinton administration strongly opposed the legislation, saying that it "will increase illegal immigration, it will reduce job opportunities for legal U.S. farm workers, and it will undercut wages and working conditions." Quoted in "Congress: Guest Workers," *Rural Migration News* 4, no. 4 (1998).

12. "No Guest Workers," *Rural Migration News* 7, no. 1 (2001). http://migration.ucdavis.edu/rmn/more_entireissue.php?idate=2001_01&number=1.

13. Ginger Thompson and Steven Greenhouse, "Mexican 'Guest Workers': A Project Worth a Try?" *New York Times*, April 3, 2001.

14. "Guest Workers: Mexico-U.S. Negotiations," *Rural Migration News* 7, no. 2 (2001). http://migration.ucdavis.edu/rmn/more_entireissue.php?idate=2001_04&number=2.

15. Quoted in "Terrorism, Guest Workers," *Rural Migration News* 7, no. 4 (2001). http://migration.ucdavis.edu/rmn/more_entireissue.php?idate=2001_10&number=4.

16. "Guest Workers: Mexico-U.S. Negotiations," *Rural Migration News* 7, no. 2 (2001).

17. Quoted in "Terrorism, Guest Workers," *Rural Migration News* 7, no. 4 (2001).

18. Quoted in "Legalization for Mexican Workers?" *Rural Migration News* 8, no. 4 (2002). http://migration.ucdavis.edu/rmn/more_entireissue.php?idate=2002_10&number=4.

19. Applications for TRS could be filed within the United States or at U.S. ports of entry with Mexico. To avoid dealing directly with the Department of Homeland Security, unauthorized foreigners could file their applications with qualified designated entities or licensed attorneys.

20. At that time, spouses and minor children of adjusting TRS immigrants could also receive immigrant visas, regardless of queues and waiting lists.

21. Rental market data from U.S. Department of Housing and Urban Development, "Fair Market Rents," 2004. http://www.huduser.org/datasets/fmr/fmrover.doc (published annually).

22. Quoted in "Bush: Legalization, AgJOBS," *Migration News* 11, no. 1 (2004). http://migration.ucdavis.edu/mn/more.php?id=2967_0_2_0.

23. Quoted in "Bush: Unauthorized, Guest Workers," *Migration News* 12, no. 2 (2005). http://migration.ucdavis.edu/mn/more_entireissue.php?idate=2005_04&number=2.

24. Quoted in "Bush: Legalization, AgJOBS," *Migration News* 11, no. 1 (2004).

25. "Congress: AgJOBS, Dream, Solve," *Migration News* 11, no. 3 (2004). http://migration.ucdavis.edu/mn/more_entireissue.php?idate=2004_07&number=3.

Chapter 8. Importing Workers, Integrating Immigrants

1. These data are from the Consumer Expenditure Survey (http://www.bls.gov/cex/); 2002 data were the most recent available on June 6, 2005.

2. Spending on processed fruits averaged $116 and on processed vegetables, $84.

3. The calculations are 0.16 x $178 = $28.48 and 0.19 x $175 = $33.25, for a total of $61.73. Data on farm–retail price spreads are at http://www.ers.usda.gov/Briefing/FoodPriceSpreads/spreads/.

4. The National Survey of America's Families defined working families as those where adults worked at least half time on average during 2001.

5. One source of such industry-transforming funds could be the employer share of Social Security and unemployment insurance taxes, which would otherwise go into general funds.

Appendix

1. Our analysis of errors from these regressions found very low correlations between the residuals from the 3SLS estimation of the farm employment and immigration equations and those from the OLS-estimated poverty equation. This supports the estimation approach used here.

REFERENCES

California Department of Food and Agriculture. 2005. "California Agricultural Statistics." Annual. http://www.nass.usda.gov/ca/bul/agstat/indexcas.htm.

California Senate. 1961, 1963. *California's Farm Labor Problems,* Parts I and II. Report of the Senate Fact Finding Committee on Labor and Welfare. Sacramento: California Senate.

Capps, Randy, Jeffrey S. Passel and Michael Fix. 2003. "A Profile of the Low-Wage Immigrant Workforce." Immigrant Families and Workers Brief 4. Washington, DC: The Urban Institute.

Carter, Colin, Darrell Hueth, John Mamer, and Andrew Schmitz. 1981. "Labor Strikes and the Price of Lettuce." *Western Journal of Agricultural Economics* 6(1): 1–14.

Carroll, Daniel, Ruth M. Samardick, Scott Bernard, Susan Gabbard, and Trish Hernandez. 2005. "Findings from the National Agricultural Workers Survey (NAWS) 2001–2002: A Demographic and Employment Profile of United States Farm Workers." Research Report No. 9. Washington, DC: Office of Programmatic Policy, Office of the Assistant Secretary for Policy, U.S. Department of Labor.

CAW. See Commission on Agricultural Workers.

Commission on Agricultural Workers. 1993. *Final Report.* Washington, DC: Government Printing Office.

Craig, Richard B. 1971. *The Bracero Program: Interest Groups and Foreign Policy.* Austin: University of Texas Press.

Daniel, Cletus E. 1981. *Bitter Harvest: A History of California Farmworkers 1870–1941.* Berkeley: University of California Press.

DOL. See U.S. Department of Labor.

Fisher, Lloyd. 1953. *The Harvest Labor Market in California.* Cambridge, MA: Harvard University Press.

Fix, Michael, and Jeffrey S. Passel. 2002. "The Scope and Impact of Welfare Reform's Immigrant Provisions." *Assessing the New Federalism* Discussion Paper 02-03. Washington, DC: The Urban Institute.

Fogel, Robert, and Stanley Engerman. 1974. *Time on the Cross: The Economics of American Negro Slavery*. Boston: Little Brown.

Fuller, Varden. 1939/1940. "The Supply of Agricultural Labor as a Factor in the Evolution of Farm Organization in California." Unpublished Ph.D. dissertation, University of California, Berkeley. Reprinted in The LaFollette Committee, *Violations of Free Speech and the Rights of Labor* (19778–894). Washington, DC: Senate Education and Labor Committee.

Fuller, Varden, and John Mamer. 1978. "Constraints on California Farm Worker Unionization." *Industrial Relations* 17(2): 143–55.

Galarza, Ernesto. 1977. *The Tragedy at Chualar*. Santa Barbara, CA: McNally and Loftin.

GAO. See General Accounting Office.

General Accounting Office. 1998. *H-2A Agricultural Guestworker Program: Experiences of Individual Vidalia Onion Growers*. GAO/HEHS-98-236R. Washington, DC: GAO.

Hahamovitch, Cindy. 1997. *The Fruits of Their Labor: Atlantic Coast Farmworkers and the Making of Migrant Poverty, 1870–1945*. Chapel Hill: The University of North Carolina Press.

Harrington, Michael. 1962. *The Other America. Poverty in the United States*. New York: Scribner.

Hasey, Janine, Roger Duncan, Heidi Sanders, Bob Beede, Maxwell Norton, Joe Grant, Bill Olson, Karen Klonsky, and Pete Livingston. 1998. "1998 Sample Costs to Establish a Cling Peach Orchard and Produce Cling Peaches." PH-SJ-98. Davis: Department of Agricultural and Resource Economics, University of California, Davis.

Limerick, Patricia Nelson. 1987. *The Legacy of Conquest: The Unbroken Past of the American West*. New York: Norton.

Lloyd, Jack, Philip L. Martin, and John Mamer. 1988. "The Ventura Citrus Labor Market." Giannini Information Series 88-1. Berkeley: Giannini Foundation of Agricultural Economics, Division of Agriculture and Natural Resources, University of California, Berkeley.

MacDonald, James M., and Michael Ollinger. 2000. "Consolidation in Meatpacking: Causes and Concerns." *Agricultural Outlook*, June–July: 23–26. Washington, DC: Economic Research Service, U.S. Department of Agriculture.

Martin, Philip L. 1994. "Good Intentions Gone Awry: IRCA and U.S. Agriculture." *The Annals of the Academy of Political and Social Science* 534: 44–57.

———. 2001. "Imperial Valley: Agriculture and Farm Labor." Paper presented at the Changing Face Conference on Imperial Valley, Holtville, California, January 16–18.

———. 2003. *Promise Unfulfilled: Unions, Immigration, and Farm Workers*. Ithaca, NY: Cornell University Press.

———. 2005. "AgJOBS. New Solution or New Problem." *UC Davis Law Review* 38(3): 973–91.

Martin, Philip L., and David Martin. 1993. *The Endless Quest: Helping America's Farm Workers*. Boulder, CO: Westview Press.

Martin, Philip L., and Alan Olmstead. 1985. "The Agricultural Mechanization Controversy." *Science* 227(4,687): 601–6.

Martin, Philip L., and J. Edward Taylor. 2003. "Farm Employment, Immigration, and Poverty: A Structural Analysis." *Journal of Agricultural and Resource Economics* 28(2): 349–63.

O'Brien, Michael, Burton Cargill, and Robert Fridley. 1983. "Principles and Practices for Harvesting and Handling Fruits and Nuts." Westport, CT: AVI Publishing.

Ollinger, Michael, James MacDonald, and Milton Madison. 2000. *Structural Change in U.S. Chicken and Turkey Slaughter*. Agricultural Economic Report 787. Washington, DC: Economic Research Service, U.S. Department of Agriculture.

President's Commission on Migratory Labor. 1951. "Migratory Labor in American Agriculture." Washington, DC: U.S. Government Printing Office.

Smith, Leslie W., and Robert Coltrane. 1981. "Hired Farmworkers: Background and Trends for the Eighties." Rural Development Research Report 32. Washington, DC: Economic Research Service, U.S. Department of Agriculture.

Steinbeck, John. 1939. *The Grapes of Wrath*. New York: Viking Penguin, Inc.

Suro, Roberto. 2005. "Survey of Mexican Migrants, Part One." Washington, DC: Pew Hispanic Center. http://pewhispanic.org/reports/report.php?ReportID=41.

Taylor, J. Edward, Philip Martin, and Michael Fix. 1997. *Poverty Amid Prosperity: Immigration and the Changing Face of Rural California*. Washington, DC: Urban Institute Press.

U.S. Congress. House of Representatives. Committee on Agriculture, Subcommittee on Equipment, Supplies, and Manpower. 1963. *Mexican Farm Labor Program*. Washington, DC: U.S. Government Printing Office.

U.S. Congress. Senate. Committee on Labor and Human Resources. 1979. *Farmworker Collective Bargaining*. 96th Cong., 1st sess.

U.S. Congress. Senate. Committee on the Judiciary. 1980. *Temporary Worker Programs: Background and Issues*. 96th Cong., 2nd sess., February.

U.S. Department of Agriculture, National Agricultural Statistics Service. 2002. "Farm Labor." http://usda.mannlib.cornell.edu/reports/nassr/other/pfl-bb/.

U.S. Department of Health and Human Services. 2005. "The 2005 HHS Poverty Guidelines." http://aspe.hhs.gov/poverty/05poverty.shtml.

U.S. Department of Labor. 1959. "Mexican Farm Labor Program." Consultants Report. Washington, DC: U.S. Department of Labor.

———. 1985–2000. *Annual Report*. Washington, DC: U.S. Department of Labor, Employment and Training Administration.

U.S. Immigration and Naturalization Service. 1991. *Statistical Yearbook of the Immigration and Naturalization Service, 1990*. Washington, DC: U.S. Government Printing Office.

ABOUT THE AUTHORS

Philip Martin is a labor economist in the Department of Agricultural and Resource Economics at the University of California, Davis. After graduating from the University of Wisconsin–Madison, he worked at the Brookings Institution and the U.S. Department of Labor, focusing on labor and immigration issues. He has worked for the World Bank, International Monetary Fund, and United Nations in many countries around the world and is the author of numerous articles and books on labor and immigration issues. Martin's research focuses on farm labor and rural poverty, labor migration and economic development, and immigration policy and guest worker issues; he has testified before Congress and state and local agencies numerous times on these issues. He is the editor of *Migration News* and *Rural Migration News* (http://migration.ucdavis.edu), and received UCD's Distinguished Public Service award in 1994.

Michael Fix is vice president and director of studies at the Migration Policy Institute, an independent think tank on national and international migration issues located in Washington, D.C. Before joining MPI in January 2005, Mr. Fix was director of immigration studies at the Urban Institute. Mr. Fix's research has focused on immigration and immigrant integration policy, race and the measurement of discrimination, federalism, and regulatory reform. Mr. Fix's recent immigration and immigrant policy research focuses on social rights and citizenship, immigrant education, and the impact of immigrants on the U.S. labor force. His recent publications include "A Profile of the Low-Wage

Immigrant Labor Force"; *Overlooked and Underserved: Immigrant Students in U.S. Secondary Schools;* and "All Under One Roof: Mixed-Status Families in an Age of Reform." He is currently working on a study of the implementation of the No Child Left Behind Act and English language learners.

J. Edward Taylor is a professor of agricultural and resource economics and director of the Center on Rural Economies of the Americas and Pacific Rim at the University of California, Davis. His recent research integrates household and general-equilibrium modeling to address questions related to rural market imperfections; population, migration, and labor supply; poverty and income inequality; technology adoption; and the environment. He also researches U.S. farm labor and rural poverty.

INDEX